# Student Motivation in English-Medium Instruction

This book explores Japanese students' learning experiences and challenges in English-medium instruction (EMI) from motivational perspectives. Using self-determination theory (SDT) as the framework, the first part reveals unfulfillment of the three psychological the need for autonomy, competence, relatedness that cause loss of students' initial interest in learning the English language and content. The author outlines pedagogical interventions that can be implemented in order to make the learning environment better. The second half of the book shows the effects these interventions had on the fulfillment of the three psychological needs, especially the need for relatedness and autonomy. The author focuses on the importance of listening to Japanese students' voices and building a community that can motivate students, thus maximizing the pedagogical effectiveness of EMI. This volume will be useful to anyone involved in motivation, language learning, or EMI research, pedagogy, or practice.

**Naoko Kojima** is Associate Professor of Applied Linguistics at Ritsumeikan University, Osaka, Japan.

T0347961

# Routledge Focus on English Medium Instruction in Higher Education

The series pulls together experts from around the world who are at the cutting edge of research on EMI within higher education. It presents a balance of research-oriented voices and evidence-based practical guidance for EMI implementation. Contributions will address the phenomenon of EMI from a range of international contexts.

As EMI research and practice is growing quickly, the Routledge Focus short-form format is the ideal platform for this series. The books in the series will focus on contemporary developments in the field, providing concise, up-to-the-minute perspectives and examples to those involved in EMI planning and implementation.

**Series Editors: Annette Bradford and Howard Brown**

**Professional Development for EMI Faculty in Mexico**
The case of Bilingual, International, and Sustainable Universities
*Myrna Escalona Sibaja*

**The Secret Life of English-Medium Instruction in Higher Education**
Examining Microphenomena in Context
*Edited by David Block and Sarah Khan*

**Student Motivation in English-Medium Instruction**
Empirical Studies in a Japanese University
*Naoko Kojima*

**Supporting EMI Students Outside of the Classroom**
Evidence from Japan
*Rachael Ruegg*

To access the full list of titles, please visit: www.routledge.com/Routledge-Focus-on-English-Medium-Instruction-in-Higher-Education/book-series/RFEHE

# Student Motivation in English-Medium Instruction

Empirical Studies in a Japanese University

**Naoko Kojima**

Routledge
Taylor & Francis Group

LONDON AND NEW YORK

First published 2021
by Routledge
2 Park Square, Milton Park, Abingdon, Oxon OX14 4RN

and by Routledge
52 Vanderbilt Avenue, New York, NY 10017

*Routledge is an imprint of the Taylor & Francis Group, an informa business*

© 2021 Naoko Kojima

*British Library Cataloguing-in-Publication Data*
A catalogue record for this book is available from the British Library

*Library of Congress Cataloging-in-Publication Data*
A catalog record has been requested for this book

ISBN: 978-0-367-25285-4 (hbk)
ISBN: 978-0-367-69049-6 (pbk)
ISBN: 978-0-429-28698-8 (ebk)

Typeset in Times New Roman
by Newgen Publishing UK

# Contents

*List of figures*     vii
*List of tables*     viii

**1    Introduction**     3

*Defining EMI and differences from CBI/CLIL 3*
*Aims of the book and data collection procedure 6*
*Contextual background 7*
*Structure of the book 9*

**2    Why motivation in EMI?**     13

*Perceptions of and motivations for EMI overseas 13*
*Perceptions of and motivations for EMI in Japanese
    universities 14*
*What is motivation? 16*
*Overview of research in second language acquisition (SLA) 17*
*A first look at motivation at University A 18*
*Theoretical framework 19*
*The gap between expectations and reality of EMI classrooms 23*

**3    Two faces of EMI motivation: Learning English and content**     30

*Study 1: A quantitative study to uncover what EMI
    motivation is 30*
*The significance of motivation to learn English, the need for
    competence and relatedness 47*

**4    How do Japanese students feel in EMI classrooms?**     50

*Study 2: The need for autonomy, competence, and
    relatedness 50*

*Designing pedagogical interventions: Inspiration from students'
comments 66*
*The necessity of pedagogical interventions 70*

**5   Pedagogical interventions to motivate students**                     72
*The pedagogical interventions from the perspective
of SDT 73*
*Study 3: Changing motivational orientations with
pedagogical interventions 76*
*The effect of the pedagogical interventions: Dependent on
motivational profiles 89*

**6   Importance of community in enhancing motivation**                    91
*Study 4: The effect of the pedagogical interventions:
Listening to students' voices 91*
*Three effective pedagogical approaches based on students'
voices 106*

**7   Conclusion: Future directions for pedagogy of EMI**                  108
*What did the studies find out? 108*
*Pedagogical implications: What can teachers and
universities do? 109*
*Final thoughts: A burden or a way to communicate
with the world? 112*

*Index*                                                                    115

# Figures

2.1 The self-determination continuum with types of
    motivation and regulation                                21
3.1 Summary of regression analyses                           40
3.2 Motivational variables for learning English for
    each cluster                                             42
3.3 EMI motivational profiles for each cluster               43
3.4 Self-reported understanding of the EMI lectures
    and self-study time for each cluster                     45
5.1 EMI intrinsic motivation for each group at
    Times 1 and 3                                            87

# Tables

| | | |
|---|---|---|
| 3.1 | Descriptive statistics for each variable in Study 1 | 34 |
| 3.2 | Correlations between motivational variables for learning English, motivational variables for learning content, and self–evaluation of background knowledge | 35 |
| 3.3 | Correlations between motivational regulations of EMI, motivational variables for learning English, and motivational variables for learning content | 37 |
| 3.4 | Correlations between the three psychological needs within the framework of SDT | 38 |
| 3.5 | Results of multiple regression analysis predicting EMI intrinsic motivation | 38 |
| 3.6 | Results of multiple regression analysis predicting EMI identified regulation | 38 |
| 3.7 | Results of multiple regression analysis predicting EMI intrinsic motivation | 39 |
| 3.8 | Results of multiple regression analysis predicting EMI identified regulation | 39 |
| 3.9 | Comparisons of descriptive statistics for intrinsic/ extrinsic motivation and psychological factors among the cluster | 41 |
| 3.10 | Descriptive statistics for self-reported understanding of the EMI lectures and self–study time for each cluster | 44 |
| 4.1 | Demographic information from the survey data of Study 1 | 51 |
| 4.2 | List of categories and concepts | 53 |
| 5.1 | Overview of class schedule, intervention, and data collection | 79 |
| 5.2 | Descriptive statistics for each factor at Time 1 (Pre-Survey) | 83 |

5.3   Descriptive statistics for each factor at Time 3
      (Post-Survey)                                        84
5.4   Descriptive statistics for participants' self-reported
      understanding of the EMI lectures                    85
5.5   Descriptive statistics for self-study time per week  85
5.6   Score of EMI intrinsic motivation for each group     85
6.1   Individual information from Study 3                   93

# Acknowledgments

I would like to begin by thanking three people in particular who have played a major role in the publication of this book. First, I would like to show my gratitude to the editors of this Focus series, Annette Bradford and Howard Brown, who encouraged and supported me from the beginning. I would also like to thank the editor at Routledge, Katie Peace, who patiently supported me to make this happen.

My deepest appreciation goes to Professor Tomoko Yashima of Kansai University, who has been one of my ideal selves as a researcher and an educator. Without her incredible patience and warm heart, this project and of course, the book, would have never seen the light of the day.

Moreover, I must acknowledge my teachers at Gonzaga University in Spokane, Washington, especially, Heidi Doolittle and Mary Jeannot, who inspired me to become a language teacher. Without any doubt, the studying abroad experience at Gonzaga University changed my life and, ever since, my journey has been full of challenges and excitements.

I want to extend a final, most sincere note of thanks to all those who agreed to take surveys, be interviewed, and share their personal experiences in classrooms. This book would not have existed without your generosity and openness. Although survey data were analyzed statistically, and pseudonyms were used throughout, I hope you feel that your voice has been heard when reading the book.

"Young people are more intelligent than adults generally give them credit for." (Csikszentmihalyi, 1997, p. 77)

# 1    Introduction

"Why do Japanese students give up so quickly?" "It seems like there are two campuses at one university. The first campus has a good group of international students, and the other one has a less smart group of Japanese students who have no intention to learn."

These were some of the comments made by the English-medium instruction (EMI) disciplinary instructors of Japanese students in EMI courses at the research site in this book (hereafter University A). It was quite disappointing for me, as an English-language instructor myself at the time, to hear these instructors' low evaluation of their students. It made me wonder whether any students would try their best and persevere with demanding courses if their instructors did not believe in their potential. After hearing more critical comments about Japanese students in EMI courses from several other EMI disciplinary instructors there, I decided to find out what was happening to the Japanese students and to explore ways to support them. Investigating language learners' motivation in EMI contexts will help Japanese students not only at University A, but also other institutions across Japan, given that EMI is becoming an "unstoppable phenomenon" and will soon be the new normal in tertiary education worldwide (Walkinshaw et al., 2017, p. 2).

## Defining EMI and differences from CBI/CLIL

### *What is EMI?*

EMI refers to "the use of the English language to teach academic subjects in countries or jurisdictions where the first language (L1) of the majority of the population is not English" (Dearden, 2015, p. 4). EMI has been increasingly implemented in higher education as English has become the de facto global language (Coleman, 2006; Crystal,

2003; Keeling, 2006). The five major characteristics of EMI, which are important to understand the definition of EMI used in this book, are as follows:

(a) EMI only uses English as the medium of instruction (i.e., not any other language such as French or German).
(b) Its main objective is content learning, so a language-learning curriculum rarely exists.
(c) It is mostly taught by disciplinary instructors with little to no experience of teaching language learners, or no professional training to do so.
(d) It is mostly implemented at the level of higher education.
(e) It includes some students who are native or near-native speakers of English.

While EMI has been widely adopted in Europe only since the 1990s, the target language (hereafter TL) has been used as a medium of instruction in language learning, including content-based instruction (CBI), since as far back the 1960s.

### *What is CBI/CLIL?*

CBI is "the concurrent study of language and subject matter, with the form and sequence of language presentation dictated by content material" (Brinton et al., 1989, p. vii). It is usually associated with immersion programs in Canada, and the balance of emphasis between language instruction and content instruction in one course can vary (Stoller, 2008).

Research on CBI has been conducted for long enough to infer that, in terms of pedagogical effectiveness, CBI has a positive impact on both language and disciplinary learning (e.g., Kasper, 1994; Rodgers, 2006; Tsai & Shang, 2010; Winter, 2004). However, some more recent studies argue that the pedagogical effectiveness of having dual objectives is open to debate (Chang, 2010; Doiz et al., 2014; Wilkinson, 2005).

Content and language integrated learning (hereafter CLIL) is "a dual-focused educational approach in which an additional language is used for the learning and teaching of both content and language" (Coyle et al., 2010, p. 1). CLIL originated in Europe, where English has often been used as a medium of instruction in CLIL classrooms (Dalton-Puffer, 2007).

Many studies have discussed whether CBI and CLIL need to be considered separately or not (e.g., Brown & Bradford, 2017; Cenoz, 2015; Tedick & Cammarata, 2012; Watanabe et al., 2011). In fact, the differences between CBI and CLIL arise not so much from pedagogical practices but rather their historical background (Paran, 2013). CBI originated in immersion programs in Canadian bilingual contexts in 1960s (Brinton et al., 1989), whereas, CLIL was rapidly developed when the EU's educational policy came into effect, which requires citizens to be competent in their mother tongue plus two additional languages (Llinares et al., 2012; Brown & Bradford, 2017). Cenoz (2015) compared CBI and CLIL from multiple perspectives in schools in the Basque Country, and concluded that they do not have any essential differences. In Japan, CBI and CLIL are often used synonymously (Brown & Bradford, 2017). In short, most of these studies conclude that CBI and CLIL are "two labels for the same reality" (Cenoz, 2015, p. 12; Coyle et al., 2010, p. 9). In line with these studies, CBI and CLIL are regarded in this book to have enough characteristics in common to be considered the same. To compare CBI/CLIL to EMI, the following (one main and four sub) aspects of CBI/CLIL need to be described:

(a) CBI/CLIL has a curriculum based on both language and content learning, so teaching practices are conducted based on these aspects;
(b) is for TL learners;
(c) in Japan, is usually taught by language teachers;
(d) includes English and other languages as TLs (e.g., German or French), and
(e) has been applied at different educational levels.

Some studies have reported the positive learning outcomes of CLIL, especially in language learning (Lasagabaster, 2008, 2011; Lorenzo et al., 2010). Sylvén and Thompson (2015) conducted a quantitative study in high schools in Sweden and found initial motivation of students in CLIL courses is already higher than students in non-CLIL courses. It means that high student motivation in CLIL courses are not necessarily the outcome of the CLIL approach, but students who are motivated tend to take CLIL. Thus, more studies have to be conducted to prove the dual pedagogical effectiveness of CLIL. Moreover, the limited learning opportunities for content in CLIL have been pointed out, as teachers are experts of either language teaching or content, but not both (Dalton-Puffer, 2007; Hoare,

2010). As described above, it is premature to conclude that CLIL is more efficient than learning language and discipline-specific content separately.

EMI is different from CBI/CLIL, yet it shares some similarities. The biggest is that stakeholders—such as policy makers, students, and even their parents—presume that students improve their English proficiency "naturally" when learning the course content in English because of the amount of exposure they get (Coleman, 2006; Swain, 1996).

In reality, however, comprehending lectures entirely in English is extremely tough for students with limited English proficiency and/or little experience learning in English. This could be a cause of motivation loss and negative attitudes toward EMI, even leading to some students dropping out. This means that EMI courses are facing serious motivation problems. As English is becoming the lingua franca in academia and EMI is becoming a new normal in tertiary education (Walkinshaw et al., 2017), dissecting EMI classrooms from a viewpoint of student motivation is an urgent matter in order to protect student learning opportunities. Consequently, various stakeholders will benefit from this book, including administrators who are unfamiliar with classroom proceedings and EMI disciplinary instructors who are aware that their EMI classrooms do not go as planned but do not know why or how to improve them (O'Dowd, 2018). In addition, the book is beneficial for language instructors as they can help EMI disciplinary instructors with methodological input to teach language learners (Macaro et al., 2019). Further, the book documents the oft-overlooked opinions of Japanese students. Japanese students are not trained to be critical of authority (Hofstede, 1980), nor do they express their emotions and opinions verbally (Nakane, 2006). Yet, Japanese students constitute the majority of the EMI student body in Japan (Shimauchi, 2016), so they must be treated as important and their opinions as essential to formulating successful EMI programs. Thus, this book attempts to make their voices heard regarding the learning experience in EMI classrooms and thereby empower them.

## Aims of the book and data collection procedure

The studies underlying this book have a twofold aim, with the following specific objectives:

(1) To understand the current situation and challenges that EMI is facing from the perspectives of Japanese students' motivation;

(2) to design and implement a series of pedagogical interventions and examine its effectiveness as a possible solution to the problems explored in the first half of this book.

In order to achieve the aim of this book, a series of the empirical studies was conducted at University A from the academic year 2014 to 2016. To produce a fuller picture of the current issues and challenges of EMI from Japanese student perspectives, mixed-method approaches were applied (Dörnyei, 2007; Van de Mieroop, 2005). It is essential to grasp the reality of EMI classrooms to determine its costs and benefits and to find a way to maximize its benefits from Japanese students' perspectives.

In each study, students were informed about the aims of the research, and that participation was voluntary and would not negatively affect their grades in any way. For the quantitative studies, they were further informed that their answers would be statistically analyzed, so that individuals could not be identified via their answers. For qualitative studies, they were informed that the data would be presented in a way that individuals could not be identified, such as by using pseudonyms. In addition, all student interviews were recorded with their explicit consent. Participants signed the consent form if they agreed.

## Contextual background

University A is a private institution in southeast Japan, founded in 2000 as one of Japan's first Japanese–English bilingual universities. Since then, it has been a driving force for the internationalization of tertiary education in the country. The university was chosen as the research site because it has implemented EMI across the university since its establishment. Since many institutions are pressured to increase the number of EMI courses, sharing what University A is experiencing could be tremendously beneficial.

At the time of the research, more than 50 percent of its full-time professors were from overseas, and about half the students were international students, mainly from Asian countries such as Vietnam, South Korea, and China. To recruit this international student population, University A offers its entrance exam in Japanese and English. Students who take the exam in Japanese are categorized as "Japanese-based students" (hereafter Japanese students), while those who take it in English are classified as "English-based students"; 90 percent of the university's undergraduate courses are offered in Japanese and English, so students can choose the medium of instruction for learning.

### The English language program

All Japanese students at University A have to undergo a placement test (the TOEFL ITP) soon after their enrollment. Students scoring lower than 500 are registered for a compulsory English language course. The students are assigned to one of the four levels based on their test scores: upper-intermediate (TOEFL ITP 500–480), intermediate (479–460), pre-intermediate (459–420), and elementary (419 or less). When they pass the upper intermediate level, they are expected to have achieved English proficiency equivalent to a TOEFL ITP score of 500. To graduate, Japanese students have to take 20 EMI credits in addition to the credits from English language-learning courses.

### EMI as a prerequisite to graduate

University A offers EMI preparatory courses and regular EMI courses. The EMI preparatory courses are exclusively for Japanese students who completed the pre-intermediate English language course. Regular EMI courses are geared toward both Japanese and international students. To take regular EMI courses, the Japanese students have to first complete the intermediate level English-language course. Students can earn a maximum of 6 of the required 20 credits from EMI preparatory courses, while the remaining 14 credits have to be earned by taking regular EMI courses.

In this book, both the regular and preparatory EMI courses are considered the same from a pedagogical point of view for the following four reasons. First, both types of courses are taught by disciplinary instructors with little to no training regarding teaching language learners. Second, because of the above, language instruction is rarely provided in either course. Third, both types are large lecture classes with a maximum of 250 students. (For example, the EMI courses in which the pedagogical interventions are carried out include more than two hundred students for Gender Studies and more than a hundred students for Cultural Studies.) Finally, there are no standard curricula, and the EMI disciplinary instructors determine the objectives and the levels of difficulty of the courses. Therefore, the EMI preparatory courses and the regular EMI courses are, for the purposes of this book, considered to fall under the same category. The first small study to look at motivation at University A, which is introduced in Chapter 2, is conducted in an EMI preparatory course (International Relations), some of the data collected in a larger-scale quantitative study in Chapter 3 (Study 1) are from another EMI pre-paratory course (e.g., Communication Studies), and the rest of the studies are conducted in regular EMI courses.

## Structure of the book

This book includes seven chapters with a series of empirical studies. After this introductory chapter defining EMI and outlining the context for the studies in this book, Chapter 2, entitled "Why motivation in EMI?" is mostly dedicated to a literature review, but also introduces the theoretical framework, self-determination theory (SDT) (Deci & Ryan, 1985), which is used throughout the book, as well as the L2 motivational self system (Dörnyei, 2005) which is applied to assess motivation to learn English.

Chapter 3, entitled "Two faces of EMI motivation: Learning English and content" discusses Study 1, a larger-scale quantitative study to understand what EMI motivation is and identify factors which influence EMI motivation. The study also compares the differences between students with higher motivation and lower motivation.

Chapter 4 is entitled "How do Japanese students feel in EMI classrooms?" and includes a qualitative study to listen to Japanese students' voices (Study 2). Specifically, Study 2 was conducted in response to Study 1 in order to explore whether or not students' three psychological needs within SDT (i.e., the need for autonomy, competence, and relatedness) were fulfilled. At the end of the chapter, students' preferred teaching approaches to design a series of pedagogical interventions to tackle this harsh learning environment in EMI classrooms are introduced.

Chapter 5, entitled "Pedagogical interventions to motivate students," first elaborates the pedagogical interventions to boost students' comprehension of the lecture and fulfill the three psychological needs within SDT, and thereby motivate them. Then, another quantitative study to explore the influence of the pedagogical interventions was reported.

Chapter 6, entitled "Importance of community in enhancing motivation," discusses a qualitative study to understand student individual learning experiences during the pedagogical interventions.

Chapter 7, entitled "Conclusion: Future directions for pedagogy of EMI," summarizes all the results and discussions in each study and suggests pedagogical implications to help Japanese students broaden their minds through taking EMI.

# References

Brinton, D. M., Snow, M. A., & Wesche, M. B. (1989). *Content-based second language instruction.* Heinle and Heinle.

Brown, H., & Bradford, A. (2017). EMI, CLIL, & CBI: Differing approaches and goals. In P. Clements, A. Krause, & H. Brown (Eds.), *Transformation in language education* (pp. 328–334). JALT.

Cenoz, J. (2015). Content-based instruction and content and language integrated learning: The same or different? *Language, Culture and Curriculum, 28*(1), 8–24. https://doi.org/10.1080/07908318.2014.1000922

Chang, Y. (2010). English-medium instruction for subject courses in tertiary education: Reactions from Taiwanese undergraduate students. *Taiwan International ESP Journal, 2,* 53–82. http://dx.doi.org/10.6706%2fTIESPJ.2010.2.1.3

Coleman, J. (2006). English-medium teaching in European higher education. *Language Teaching, 39*(1), 1–14. https://doi.org/10.1017/S02614448 0600320X

Coyle, D., Hood, P., & Marsh, D. (2010). *Content and language integrated learning.* Cambridge University Press.

Crystal, D. (2003). *English as a global language* (2nd ed.). Cambridge University Press. https://doi.org/10.1017/CBO9780511486999

Csikszentmihalyi, M. (1997). Intrinsic motivation and effective teaching: A flow analysis. In J. L. Bess (Ed.), *Teaching well and liking it: Motivating faculty to teach effectively* (pp. 72–89). Johns Hopkins University Press.

Dalton-Puffer, C. (2007). *Discourse in content and language integrated (CLIL) classrooms.* John Benjamins. https://doi.org/10.1075/lllt.20

Dearden, J. (2015). *English as a medium of instruction—A growing global phenomenon.* https://www.britishcouncil.org/education/lhe/knowledge-centre/English-language-higher-education/report-english-medium-instruction

Deci, E. L., & Ryan, R. M. (1985). *Intrinsic motivation and self-determination in human behavior.* Plenum.

Doiz, A., Lasagabaster, D., & Sierra, J. M. (2014). CLIL and motivation: The effect of individual and contextual variables. *The Language Learning Journal, 42*(2), 209–224. https://doi.org/10.1080/09571736.2014.889508

Dörnyei, Z. (2005). *The psychology of the language learner: Individual differences in second language acquisition.* Routledge. https://doi.org/10.4324/9781410613349

Dörnyei, Z. (2007). *Research methods in applied linguistics.* Oxford University Press.

Hoare, P. (2010). Content-based language teaching in China: Contextual influences on implementation. *Journal of Multilingual and Multicultural Development, 31*(1), 69–86. https://doi.org/10.1080/01434630903367207

Hofstede, G. (1980). *Culture's consequences: International differences in work-related values.* Sage.

Kasper, L. F. (1994). Improved reading performance for ESL students through academic course pairing. *Journal of Reading, 37*(5), 376–384.

Keeling, R. (2006). The Bologna Process and the Lisbon Research Agenda: The European Commission's expanding role in higher education discourse. *European Journal of Education, 41*(2), 203–223. https://doi.org/10.1111/j.1465-3435.2006.00256.x

Lasagabaster, D. (2008). Foreign language competence in content and language integrated courses. *The Open Applied Linguistics Journal, 1*, 30–41. http://dx.doi.org/10.2174/1874913500801010030

Lasagabaster, D. (2011). English achievement and student motivation in CLIL and EFL settings. *Innovation in Language Learning and Teaching, 5*(1), 3–18. https://doi.org/10.1080/17501229.2010.519030

Llinares, A., Morton, T., & Whittaker, R. (2012). *The role of language in CLIL.* Cambridge University Press.

Lorenzo, F., Casal, S., & Moore, P. (2010). The effects of content and language integrated learning in European education: Key findings from Andalusian sections evaluation project. *Applied Linguistics, 31*(3), 418–442. https://doi.org/10.1093/applin/amp041

Macaro, D., Jimenez-Munoz, A., & Lasagabaster, D. (2019). The importance of certification of English medium instruction teachers in higher education in Spain. *Porta Linguarum, 32*, 103–118.

Nakane, I. (2006). Silence and politeness in intercultural communication in university seminars. *Journal of Pragmatics, 38*(11), 1811–1835. https://doi.org/10.1016/j.pragma.2006.01.005

O'Dowd, R. (2018). The training and accreditation of teachers for English medium instruction: An overview of practice in European universities. *International Journal of bilingual education and bilingualism, 21*(5), 553–563. https://doi.org/10.1080/13670050.2018.1491945

Paran, A. (2013). Content and language integrated learning: Panacea or policy borrowing myth? *Applied Linguistics Review, 4*(2), 317–342. https://doi.org/10.1515/applirev-2013-0014

Rodgers, D. M. (2006). Developing content and form: Encouraging evidence from Italian content-based instruction. *The Modern Language Journal, 90*(3), 373–386. https://doi.org/10.1111/j.1540-4781.2006.00430.x

Shimauchi, S. (2016). *Higashi Ajia ni okeru ryugakusei ido no paradaimu tenkan: Daigaku kokusaika to 'Eigo puroguramu' no hikkan hikaku* [Paradigm shift on international student mobility in East Asia: Comparative analysis on internationalization of higher education and English-medium degree programs in Japan and South Korea]. Toshindo.

Stoller, F. L. (2008). Content-based instruction. In N. H. Hornberger (Ed.), *Encyclopedia of language and education* (pp. 1163–1174). Springer.

Swain, M. (1996). Integrating language and content in immersion classrooms: Research perspectives. *Canadian Modern Language Review, 52*(4), 529–548. https://doi.org/10.3138/cmlr.52.4.529

Sylvén, L, K., & Thompson, A, S. (2015). Language learning motivation and CLIL: Is there a connection? *Journal of Immersion and Content-Based Language Education, 3*(1), 28–50. https://doi.org/10.1075/jicb.3.1.02syl

Tedick, D. J., & Cammarata, L. (2012). Content and language integration in K-12 contexts: Student outcomes, teacher practices, and stakeholder perspectives. *Foreign Language Annals*, *45*(s1), s28–s53. https://doi.org/10.1111/j.1944-9720.2012.01178.x

Tsai, Y., & Shang, H. (2010). The impact of content-based language instruction on EFL students' reading performance. *Asian Social Science*, *6*(3), 77–85. https://doi.org/10.5539/ass.v6n3p77

Van de Mieroop, D. (2005). An integrated approach of quantitative and qualitative analysis in the study of identity in speeches. *Discourse & Society*, *16*(1), 107–130. https://doi.org/10.1177/0957926505048232

Walkinshaw, I., Fenton-Smith, B., & Humphreys, P. (2017). EMI issues and challenges in Asia-Pacific higher education: An introduction. In B. Fenton-Smith, P. Humphreys, & I. Walkinshaw (Eds.), *English medium instruction in higher education in Asia-Pacific: From policy to pedagogy* (pp. 1–18). Springer.

Watanabe, Y., & Ikeda, M., & Izumi, S. (2011). *CLIL (Content and language integrated learning): New challenges in foreign language education at Sophia University*. Sophia University Press.

Wilkinson, R. (2005). *The impact of language on teaching content*: Views from the content teacher. Retrieved 21 December 2011 www.palmenia. helsinki.fi/congress/bilingual2005 presentations/wilkinson.pdf

Winter, W. E. (2004). The performance of ESD students in a content-linked psychology course. *Community Review*, *18*, 76–82.

# 2 Why motivation in EMI?

## Perceptions of and motivations for EMI overseas

As mentioned in Chapter 1, there is not enough research to prove the pedagogical effectiveness of English-medium instruction (EMI) (Macaro, 2018). There is an assumption of having dual pedagogical effectiveness—improving students' English proficiency while they acquire new knowledge. However, even content and language integrated learning (CLIL), which has the express goal of teaching both content and language, requires more research to conclude its pedagogical effectiveness (Chang, 2010; Macaro, 2018; Wilkinson, 2005). Therefore, it is easy to imagine that EMI is facing similar—or even more severe—challenges to CLIL in enhancing both students' language and content learning.

Although EMI's pedagogical effectiveness has not yet been confirmed, some research has demonstrated that students' assumptions about its dual benefits (it may give them more career options) drive their initial intentions for taking EMI (Chang, 2010; Flowerdew et al., 1998; Malcolm, 2013). Further, as Gao (2008) reported based on an interview study with Chinese university students who study abroad to take classes in English, EMI helps to motivate students intrinsically to learn English. This indicates that EMI is effective, at least enhancing students' drive to learn English.

On the other hand, other research has highlighted EMI's limited pedagogical effectiveness, and even its drawbacks (Byun et al., 2011; Chang, 2010; Joe & Lee, 2013; Malcolm, 2013; Sert, 2008; Wu, 2006). In particular, studies about EMI instructors in several different contexts have reported that some of them have developed negative attitudes toward EMI. For example, EMI disciplinary instructors in Turkey feared that students who were eager to learn but had limited language proficiency could lose their self-efficacy and drive to learn because of the language barrier (Sert, 2008). In addition, EMI disciplinary instructors in Italy are concerned about their own low English proficiency, which could negatively impact students' language and content learning (Campagna, 2016; Pulcini & Campagna, 2015). In the Korean context, EMI disciplinary teachers are forced to teach EMI, but they prefer teaching in Korean since EMI reduces the amount of knowledge that they can impart and their interaction with the students (Cho, 2012). The studies discussed above show that teachers have gradually realized that EMI could decrease opportunities for students to learn and become a burden for those without high English proficiency.

Other research in South Korea explored EMI from students' perspectives and reported that students feel obligated to take EMI, especially students with lower English proficiency (Kang & Park, 2005). Joe and Lee (2013) conducted a survey project with Korean medical students and reported that even students with TOEFL ITP scores around 590, CEFR B2, were less satisfied and had a harder time following classes in English compared to the lectures in their L1: Korean. Their study did not have a control group but used only one group of participants to compare EMI and Korean-medium instruction. Therefore, the reliability of the results is not adequate for a scientific study. Nevertheless, the studies discussed above imply that although high English proficiency is necessary to encourage students to take EMI, it does not guarantee their success in the courses.

Previous EMI research also sheds light on the possible pros and cons of EMI. Teachers, students, and even parents assume that EMI is beneficial for both language and content learning although, in theory, it is not intended for language learning (Chang, 2010; Wu, 2006). However, in reality, EMI disciplinary instructors and students seemed to struggle with identifying the significance of EMI; thus, it was challenging for them to motivate themselves to teach EMI or study in EMI courses (Campagna, 2016; Cho, 2012; Joe & Lee, 2013; Pulcini & Campagna, 2015; Sert, 2008).

Compared to other parts of the world, Japan lags in EMI implementation and research (Hashimoto, 2018). Despite the limited amount of research, the following section tries to uncover how EMI is implemented and what is happening in Japanese tertiary education.

## Perceptions of and motivations for EMI in Japanese universities

In Japan, EMI has grown rapidly since 2000 with the aim of achieving the following three goals (Shimauchi, 2016, p. 65):

(a) Promote internationalization on campus to improve the international and domestic competitiveness of universities;
(b) Recruit a higher number of better-qualified international students;
(c) Increase domestic students' competitiveness in the international market (i.e., transforming domestic students into global citizens).

Due to its hasty expansion, EMI's application at Japanese universities has been somewhat uncoordinated (Bradford & Brown, 2018). Shimauchi (2016) conducted a survey including all four-year universities ($N = 760$) in Japan to uncover how EMI has been implemented, and the results revealed that 292 programs at 78 universities offer EMI, which is a slightly less than 309, the 2016 number reported by Ministry of Education, Culture, Sports, Science and Technology (MEXT) (2019). Shimauchi further investigated which level of education and majors offered EMI, and found that approximately 85 percent of EMI courses in Japan were at the graduate level and that national and public universities tended to implement EMI in science majors. On the other hand, many private universities implemented EMI in humanities majors. In total, 60 percent of EMI courses are offered to science majors (e.g., medicine, engineering, and ecology), and 40 percent to humanities majors (e.g., business, global studies, and international studies). In addition, the forms of EMI varied—some universities offered EMI across the universities, and others provided EMI classes in some specific departments (but not the entire school). Meanwhile, others integrated EMI as a part of the curriculum in a department, but Japanese was the main medium of instruction in the department.

Shimauchi (2016) also categorized EMI in Japanese universities into the following three types:

(a) The global citizen model, in which the majority (90 percent) of students are Japanese, and EMI is used to help transform students into global citizens;

(b) the crossroad model, in which domestic and international students share the learning environment (about 30–70 percent of the students are international); and

(c) the Dejima model, in which most of the students (90 percent) are from overseas and study in an isolated setting.

Many EMI programs in Japan are the first type (Shimauchi, 2016; Brown & Iyobe, 2014).

As mentioned, very few EMI studies have been conducted in Japan, and most have been carried out to understand the challenges in implementing EMI from the perspectives of institutions, and from international students' complaints about the low level and limited choice of courses (e.g., Bradford, 2013; Heigham, 2018; Shimauchi, 2016; Tsuneyoshi, 2005). Due to the lack of classroom research focusing on Japanese students, there is little knowledge about the EMI learning experiences of domestic students and the types of support that universities should provide. However, the following two studies have suggested that English learning is one of the aims that Japanese students have when they enroll for EMI courses. Shimauchi (2018) conducted an interview study with 12 Japanese students. One of the objectives of the study was to explore the reasons why they opt for EMI. The results showed that students believed EMI helps to improve their English, especially in terms of academic speaking skills (e.g., presentation skills and being able to express one's opinions), even if a course did not include international students. Likewise, Chapple (2015) conducted a longitudinal study at Japanese universities with 89 Japanese students and 26 international students. The results of surveys and interviews revealed that the Japanese students' reasons for taking EMI were mostly related to English learning, such as making international friends, and experiencing authentic English. However, in reality, it seemed challenging for them to maintain their initial motivation for EMI (Chapple, 2015; Hino, 2017). In these studies, many Japanese students dropped out of their EMI courses. Neither Chapple nor Hino revealed why the students quit, but those who survived until the end of the course stated that following the EMI lectures was a lot more demanding than they expected. Therefore, previous research on EMI suggests that students in EMI lose their motivation as a consequence of not being able to follow EMI courses. It means studies that explore students' motivation to gain a deeper understanding of EMI are essential to capture the current situation of EMI and the problems EMI faces.

## What is motivation?

Motivation is crucial to learning and is at least as critical as one's aptitude, learning environment, or intelligence (Gardner, 1985). Dörnyei and Ushioda (2011) describe motivation as a concept related to "why people decide to do something," "how long they are willing to sustain the activity," and "how hard they are going to pursue it" (p. 4). It also "provides the primary impetus to initiate L2 (second language) learning and later the driving force to sustain the long, often tedious[,] learning process" (Dörnyei & Ryan, 2015, p. 72). As previous studies have suggested, it seems that Japanese students increasingly stop attending EMI courses, which could infer that students in these EMI courses are facing serious motivation problems. In other words, exploring EMI from the viewpoint of student motivation is beneficial to understand the current situation and problems of EMI classrooms.

On the other hand, what EMI motivation actually is remains unknown. Previous research implied that students prioritize language learning over content learning when taking EMI (Chapple, 2015; Shimauchim 2018; Turhan & Kirkgöz, 2018). What keeps students going while taking EMI courses has not been sufficiently uncovered, but the students, instructors and even administrators seem to expect students will learn English incidentally in order to follow the lectures without explicit language instruction (Schmidt-Unterberger, 2018; Wilkinson, 2011). Taking this assumption into account, EMI can be considered as a part of the language learning continuum (Macaro, 2018), although language teaching is not a part of course objectives of EMI in theory. Thus, perspectives of second language acquisition (SLA) must be included when conducting research in EMI classrooms.

## Overview of research in second language acquisition (SLA)

Motivation research has attracted the interest of many SLA researchers since the 1960s and was classified into three periods (Dörnyei, 2005): (1) the social-psychological period (1959–1990), when most of the work was conducted in a Canadian bilingual context; (2) the cognitive-situated period (during the 1990s); and (3) from the process-oriented period to the socio-dynamic period (2000–present).

Self-determination theory (hereafter SDT) was brought to the SLA research field from educational psychology during the cognitive-situated period. During this period, several motivational theories in educational psychology were applied in SLA, in addition to SDT, such as goal theory and attribution theory to explore students' motivation in actual classrooms (Dörnyei & Ryan, 2015). The investigations during this period further reported that social contexts such as the teacher, classroom materials, and peers could promote, maintain, or hinder language learning.

During the third period, from the process-oriented period to the socio-dynamic period, researchers focused on time and examined motivation as a process. In this paradigm shift, a future-oriented theory, the L2 motivational self system (Dörnyei, 2005) was postulated. It became one of the most influential works of the third period. Moreover, researchers became aware of the limitations of understanding real-world motivation from a static standpoint, which drastically increased the number of studies in the field applying mixed or qualitative methods (Boo et al., 2015).

## A first look at motivation at University A

Based on the context of University A, I became interested in understanding the motivation of Japanese students in the EMI courses. In English language classrooms, Japanese students were willing to communicate with each other, share their opinions, and answer questions voluntarily in English. However, in EMI classrooms, Japanese students sat at the back of the classroom and kept silent, seemingly nonexistent. Observing this inspired me to conduct a small-scale survey and follow-up interview project with 44 Japanese students in an EMI preparatory course at University A. The results implied a change of motivation over time. At the beginning of the course, students take EMI not only as a prerequisite to graduate, but also to fulfil their desire to learn content that they are curious about in English. Nevertheless, they gradually lose their initial motivation since they cannot follow one-way lecture-style classes with hundreds of students. In fact, the results showed that on average students did not understand even half of the lectures, and 59 percent of the participants wanted to drop out of the course as it was far too demanding for them to follow. After having this kind of harsh learning experience continuously, they lose their intellectual curiosity, and attend EMI classes only out of obligation; most of them attended the course until the end simply because it was a prerequisite to graduate. In truth, the drop-out rate for the course that this study was conducted in was 44 percent.

Some stories from interviewees stood out and reflected a change in motivation. For example, one of the participants said that she took the EMI course as a preparation for studying abroad in addition to her interests in criminology. Her TOEFL ITP score improved from 490 to over 550 during the semester when she was taking the EMI preparatory course. It could be said that she was a student who had tried hard to improve her English proficiency. However, she did not understand the lectures or textbooks at all after spending hours trying to understand the course content in the EMI course. Consequently, she felt that putting in the effort to catch up with the EMI course was "a waste of time," and therefore, switched to spending her time studying for the TOEFL. She did not spend any more time on that class at the end of the course. Her internal motivation to gain the knowledge of criminology while improving her English disappeared because of constantly feeling incompetent.

This small study made it clear that students at University A in EMI are facing a motivation problem: therefore, exploring EMI from the angle of motivation is critical. The results also indicated that Japanese students are constantly feeling incompetence in EMI classrooms, which transforms their EMI motivation from autonomous to external. This implies that Deci and Ryan's (1985) SDT could be the best framework for exploring EMI motivation.

In addition, another participant in the interview studied four hours per week for the EMI preparatory course because he believed that taking the EMI course was an important step in achieving his career goal of becoming an interpreter. In other words, the intended effort to learn English, especially a clear image of a future ideal self as an English speaker, could be a driving force in EMI. In fact, an objective of EMI is to help Japanese students be competitive in this globalized world (i.e., *global jinzai*) (Brown, 2018; Yonezawa, 2011), which means they will use English to study abroad or at work in the future. Therefore, aligning the educational objectives of EMI with the results of this preliminary study suggests that the ideal L2 self and ought-to L2 self of Dörnyei's L2 motivational self system (2005) be applied to assess students' intended effort to learn English.

## Theoretical framework

### *Self-determination theory (SDT)*

SDT hypothesizes (Deci & Ryan, 1985; Ryan & Deci, 2000, 2002) that people have an innate tendency to self-regulate their behavior and engage with others for intellectual growth. However, this tendency can be enhanced or diminished depending on the environment. Within SDT, human motivation can be broadly categorized into intrinsic and extrinsic motivation (Deci & Ryan, 1985). When a student is intrinsically motivated, they perform an activity because it is exciting and enjoyable (e.g., "I am taking EMI because it is fun"). In contrast, when a student is extrinsically motivated, they perform an activity to achieve a separate goal (e.g., "I am taking EMI because I want to get a higher TOEFL score"). According to Deci and Ryan (1985) and Ryan and Deci (2000, 2002), fulfilling the three psychological needs— the need for autonomy, the need for competence, and the need for relatedness—is universal and essential for one's motivation and well-being.

The fulfillment of the need for autonomy is key to increasing intrinsic motivation and mature types of extrinsic motivation at any educational level. It is because autonomy-supportive teaching practices will lead to greater engagement, positive emotions, and greater conceptual learning (Reeve, 2002). Applying autonomy-supportive teaching approaches also helps satisfy teachers' sense of autonomy (Cheon et al., 2018). To fulfill students' need for autonomy, teachers can be responsive, supportive, and flexible. Although providing choices is the most popular way to satisfy students' sense of autonomy in English classrooms in Japan (e.g., Hiromori, 2006; Maekawa & Yashima, 2012), research has illustrated various ways to fulfill the need for perceived autonomy. For example, instructors could spend time listening to students, involve students in the learning process, explain the value or relevance of the studied materials, and take students' perspectives into consideration (Kaplan, 2018; Reeve, 2002). On the other hand, giving answers, criticizing, and motivating through pressure could decrease the satisfaction of the need for autonomy, and thus suppress the quality and strength of motivation, which causes negative outcomes (Reeve, 2002). To sum up, accepting and acknowledging students and their opinions with a non-judgmental attitude can boost their need for autonomy (Skinner & Edge, 2002).

The need for competence involves a desire to be competent in terms of one's actions, skills, and abilities (Ryan & Deci, 2002). It will be fulfilled when one has an optimal challenge with effective feedback, which leads to a sense of achievement, growth and self-efficacy (Rawsthorne & Elliot, 1999). Consequently, it would lead to strong engagement in further tasks. On the other hand, negative feedback could make the person feel that they were not good enough and were unworthy.

Finally, the need for relatedness, which is a desire to belong with other individuals and to a community, facilitates the process of the internalization of extrinsic motivation and fosters intrinsic motivation (Niemiec & Ryan, 2009; Ryan & Deci, 2002). It is cultivated when people feel connected to and supported by significant others. Satisfaction of the need for relatedness would lead to motivated behaviors such as persistence, exerting more effort, and being more confident. On the other hand, failure to fulfill the need for relatedness causes negative emotions such as fear, anxiety, and boredom. All these feelings lead to burnout and a sense of being ignored and turn people away from learning opportunities (Furrer & Skinner, 2003; Niemiec & Ryan, 2009). It means that to be engaged, have fun, and be interested in classroom activities students need to feel that their teachers appreciate them (Furrer & Skinner, 2003).

The needs for autonomy, competence, and relatedness are interconnected, yet different (Ryan & Deci, 2002). Fulfillment of all of these needs is vital and universal to enhancing intrinsic motivation and/ or autonomous types of extrinsic motivation, although the role of each need differs depends on contexts, which is also confirmed with some research in English classrooms in Japan (Hiromori, 2003, 2006).

| Amotivation | | Extrinsic motivation | | | Intrinsic motivation |
|---|---|---|---|---|---|
| | External regulation | Introjected regulation | Identified regulation | Integrated regulation | Intrinsic regulation |
| Non-self-determined | ← | | | → | Self-determined |

*Figure 2.1* The self-determination continuum with types of motivation and regulation.
*Source*: Adapted from Ryan and Deci (2000, 2002).

Deci and Ryan (1985) and Ryan and Deci (2002) also introduced a sub-theory called organismic integration theory (OIT). Within OIT, they presented four forms of extrinsic motivation—external regulation, introjected regulation, identified regulation, and integrated regulation—which have different degrees of self-determination, in addition to amotivation (see Figure 2.1). Amotivation is the state of lacking the intention to carry out an activity because one does not value the activity or feels unable to do so. In terms of extrinsic motivation, the least self-determined form is external regulation, which involves performing an action for a reward or to avoid punishment, such as attending a class to gain necessary credits. The next level of extrinsic motivation is introjected regulation, which is more internalized than external regulation; it entails carrying out an activity with the hope of receiving compliments from others or to avoid feeling guilty for not performing a certain task. Identified regulation is a more mature form of extrinsic motivation, involving the individual's recognition of an activity's value of achieving key goals. Finally, integrated regulation is the most internalized form of extrinsic motivation, and entails performing activities that are in harmony with one's identity (Ryan & Deci, 2002).

SDT first inspired SLA researchers in Canada (Noels, 2001; Noels et al., 1999; Noels et al., 2000), and much research has been conducted using SDT. In Japan, Hiromori (2003) first examined the applicability of SDT in English classrooms (see also Yashima et al., 2009). Many scholars have employed SDT in a variety of contexts, especially in interventional studies aiming to enhance student intrinsic motivation or internalize extrinsic motivation by fulfilling the three psychological needs (e.g., Agawa & Takeuchi, 2017; Hiromori, 2006; Hiromori & Tanaka, 2006; Maekawa & Yashima, 2012; Tanaka & Hiromori, 2007). There are three interventional studies in Japan that are notable for their close examination of data that enables identification of increases in motivation. First, Hiromori (2006) applied creative group writing activities to boost intrinsic motivation, which succeeded in motivating 68 percent of the participants. The percentage of participants who increased their motivation was exceptionally high compared to the other studies (which will be introduced later). Tanaka and Hiromori's (2007) study succeeded in increasing 26 percent of the participants' intrinsic motivation by using group presentation activities. Finally, Maekawa and Yashima's (2012) study among Japanese engineering students also succeeded in enhancing 22 percent of the participants intrinsic motivation by designing a presentation-based course.

It should be noted that students who demonstrated lower intrinsic motivation at the beginning of the experiment tended to develop their motivation. However, students who had high intrinsic motivation from the beginning did not increase their motivation but, rather, sustained it, as seen even in an outstanding study conducted by Hiromori (2006). This implies that it is extremely challenging to increase intrinsic motivation among students who are already motivated. Further, the previous studies introduced above showed the importance of categorizing students based on their motivational profiles because effective teaching approaches differ accordingly. As we have observed, SDT has been employed in numerous studies to understand the development of and decline in motivation among students, especially in interventional studies in Japan.

## The L2 motivational self system

Another key theoretical framework for this book is the L2 motivational self system, first conceptualized by Dörnyei (2005) based on two psychological theories: the theory of possible selves (Markus & Nurius, 1986) and the self-discrepancy theory (Higgins, 1987). According to Markus and Nurius (1986), possible selves include what one would like to become, could become, and is afraid of becoming. Self-discrepancy theory (Higgins, 1987) proposes the ideal self as a representation of the qualities that one ideally possesses and the ought self as a representation of the attributes one believes one should possess. The ideal and ought selves work as self-guides when one is trying to reduce the gap between one's actual self and one's ideal or ought self.

Dörnyei (2005) applied these theories and postulated the L2 motivational self system as a motivation theory in SLA that has three components, namely, the ideal L2 self, ought-to L2 self, and L2 learning experience. The ideal L2 self is the representation of one's ideal self as an L2 speaker. If one's ideal self speaks the L2, that image could be a great motivator in language learning as one attempts to minimize the distance between the ideal and actual selves as an L2 speaker (Dörnyei, 2009). Hence, learners who can clearly and vividly imagine their ideal selves as L2 users are more motivated for language learning. On the other hand, the ought-to L2 self is "the representation of the attributes that one believes one should possess to meet expectations or to avoid negative outcomes" (Dörnyei & Ryan, 2015, p. 87). Compared to the ideal L2 self, short-term goals, such as getting a better grade, tend to be motivators for the ought-to L2 self. Finally, the third component of the theory is L2 learning experience, whereby the immediate language learning experience and learning context to some extent affect students' motivation in language classrooms (Dörnyei, 2005).

The L2 motivational self system has remained popular among SLA researchers worldwide since its inception in 2005 (e.g., Csizér & Kormos, 2009; Maekawa & Yashima, 2012; Ryan, 2009; Taguchi et al., 2009). These studies have found that the ideal L2 self motivates students to learn English. The ought-to L2 self does motivate students, but studies in Asia have discovered its impact to be limited (e.g., Taguchi et al., 2009; Ryan, 2009; Yashima et al., 2017). Studies in Chile and Hungary have reported that it is not an influential factor (Csizér & Kormos, 2009). Some studies in Japan mention the relationship between the ideal L2 self and SDT (Konno, 2011; Nishida, 2013; Yashima, 2009). They have demonstrated that the ideal L2 self increased intrinsic motivation and helped to internalize extrinsic motivation.

## The gap between expectations and reality of EMI classrooms

Universities around the globe, including Japanese universities, have been implementing EMI as an effort to internationalize their campuses. One of the pedagogical effects that Japanese tertiary education expected is that students would learn English naturally while learning content. This would help transform domestic students into *global jinzai*. Students take EMI classes not only for their credits or future career, but also based on their desire to use English in an authentic context and to study an academic subject that they are interested in. However, in reality, students lose self-efficacy and motivation with a one-way lecture style of teaching, and some of them even drop out. Since EMI is a context in which extrinsic motivation and intrinsic motivation interplay, SDT will be applied as the main theoretical framework in the studies in this book. In addition, as EMI itself is future-oriented, students who vividly imagine themselves using English should be expected to maintain their high motivation in EMI. Thus, the ideal L2 self and ought-to L2 self of the L2 motivational self system are applied as variables to assess their motivation to learn English in EMI. Chapter 3 will discuss a larger-scale quantitative study (Study 1) to understand motivation in EMI in depth using SDT as the framework.

## References

Agawa, T., & Takeuchi, O. (2017). Pedagogical intervention to enhance self-determined forms of L2 motivation: Applying self-determination theory in the Japanese university EFL context. *Language Education & Technology, 54,* 135–166.

Boo, Z., Dörnyei, Z., & Ryan, S. (2015). L2 motivation research 2005–2014: Understanding a publication surge and a changing landscape. *System, 55,* 145–157. https://doi.org/10.1016/j.system.2015.10.006

Bradford, A. (2013). English-medium degree programs in Japanese universities: Learning from the European experience. *Asian Education and Development Studies, 2*(3), 225–240. https://doi.org/10.1108/AEDS-06-2012-0016

Bradford, A., & Brown, H. (2018). ROAD-MAPPING English-medium instruction in Japan. In A. Bradford & H. Brown (Eds.), *English-medium instruction in Japanese higher education: Policy challenges and outcomes* (pp. 3–13). Multilingual Matters. https://doi.org/10.21832/9781783098958-004

Brown, H. (2018). English-medium instruction in Japanese universities: History and perspectives. In P. Clements, A. Krause, & P. Bennett (Eds.), *Language teaching in a global age: Shaping the classrooms, shaping the world.* JALT.

Brown, H., & Iyobe, B. (2014). The growth of English medium instruction in Japan. In N. Sonda & A. Krause (Eds.), *JALT2013 Conference Proceedings* (pp. 9–19). JALT. https://jalt-publications.org/files/pdf-article/jalt2013_002.pdf

Byun, K., Chu, H., Kim, M., Park, I., Kim, S., & Jung, J. (2011). English-medium teaching in Korean higher education: Policy debates and reality. *Higher Education, 62*(4), 431–449. https://doi.org/10.1007/s10734-010-9397-4

Campagna, S. (2016). English as a medium of instruction. A "resentment study" of a micro EMI context. In S. Campagna, E. Ochse, V. Pulcini, & M. Solly (Eds.), *"Languaging" in and across communities: New voices, new identities* (pp. 145–168). Peter Lang.

Chang, Y. (2010). English-medium instruction for subject courses in tertiary education: Reactions from Taiwanese undergraduate students. *Taiwan International ESP Journal, 2,* 53–82. http://dx.doi.org/10.6706%2fTIESPJ.2010.2.1.3

Chapple, J. (2015). Teaching in English is not necessarily the teaching of English. *International Education Studies, 8*(3), 1–13. https://doi.org/10.5539/ies.v8n3p1

Cheon, S., Reeve, J., & Ntoumanis, N. (2018). A needs-supportive intervention to help PE teachers enhance students' prosocial behavior and diminish anti-social behavior. *Psychology of Sport and Exercise, 35*, 74–88. https://doi.org/10.1016/j.psychsport.2017.11.010

Cho, D. W. (2012). English-medium instruction in the university context of Korea: Trade-off between teaching outcomes and media-initiated university ranking. *The Journal of Asia TEFL, 9*(4), 135–163.

Csizér, K., & Kormos, J. (2009). Learning experiences, selves, and motivated learning behavior: A comparative analysis of structural models for Hungarian secondary and university learners of English. In Z. Dörnyei & E. Ushioda (Eds.), *Motivation, language identity and the L2 self* (pp. 98–119). Multilingual Matters. https://doi.org/10.21832/9781847691293-006

Deci, E. L., & Ryan, R. M. (1985). *Intrinsic motivation and self-determination in human behavior.* Plenum.

Dörnyei, Z. (2005). *The psychology of the language learner: Individual differences in second language acquisition.* Routledge. https://doi.org/10.4324/9781410613349

Dörnyei, Z. (2009). The L2 motivational self system. In Z. Dörnyei & E. Ushioda (Eds.), *Motivation, language identity and the L2 self* (pp. 9–42). Multilingual Matters. https://doi.org/10.21832/9781847691293-003

Dörnyei, Z., & Ryan, S. (2015). *The psychology of the language learner revisited.* Routledge.

Dörnyei, Z., & Ushioda, E. (2011). *Teaching and researching motivation* (2nd ed.). Longman.

Flowerdew, J., Li, D., & Miller, L. (1998). Attitudes toward English and Cantonese among Hong Kong Chinese university lecturers. *TESOL Quarterly, 32*(2), 201–231. https://doi.org/10.2307/3587582

Furrer, C., & Skinner, E. (2003). Sense of relatedness as a factor in children's academic engagement and performance. *Journal of Educational Psychology, 95*(1), 148–162. https://doi.org/10.1037/0022-0663.95.1.148

Gao, X. (2008). Shifting motivational discourses among mainland Chinese students in an English medium tertiary institution in Hong Kong: A longitudinal inquiry. *Studies in Higher Education, 33*(5), 599–614. https://doi.org/10.1080/03075070802373107

Gardner, R. C. (1985). *Social psychology and second language learning: The role of attitudes and motivation.* Edward Arnold.

Hashimoto, H. (2018). Government policy driving English-medium instruction at Japanese universities: Responding to a competitiveness crisis in a globalizing world. In A. Bradford, & H. Brown (Eds.), *English-medium instruction in Japanese higher education: Policy challenges and outcomes* (pp. 14–31). Multilingual Matters. https://doi.org/10.21832/9781783098958-004

Heigham, J. (2018). Center stage but invisible: International students in an English-taught program. In A. Bradford & H. Brown (Eds.), *English-medium instruction in Japanese higher education: Policy challenges and outcomes* (pp. 161–179). Multilingual Matters. https://doi.org/10.21832/9781783098958-004

Higgins, E. T. (1987). Self-discrepancy: A theory relating self and affect. *Psychological Review*, *94*(3), 319–340. https://doi.org/10.1037/0033-295x. 94.3.319

Hino, N. (2017). The significance of EMI for the learning of EIL in higher education: Four cases from Japan. In B. Fenton-Smith, P. Humphreys, & I. Walkinshaw (Eds.), *English medium instruction in higher education in Asia-Pacific: From policy to pedagogy* (pp. 115–131). Springer.

Hiromori, T. (2003). What enhances language learners' motivation? High school English learners' motivation from the perspective of self-determination theory. *JALT Journal*, *25*(2), 173–186. https://doi.org/10.37546/JALTJJ25.2-3

Hiromori, T. (2006). The effects of educational intervention on L2 learners' motivational development. *JACET Bulletin*, *43*, 1–14.

Hiromori, T., & Tanaka, H. (2006). Instructional intervention on motivating English learners: The self-determination theory viewpoint. *Language Education and Technology*, *43*, 111–126.

Joe, Y., & Lee, H. K. (2013). Does English-medium instruction benefit students in EFL contexts? A case study of medical students in Korea. *Asia-Pacific Education Researcher*, *22*, 201–207. https://doi.org/10.1007/s40299-012-0003-7

Kang, S., & H. Park (2005). English as the medium of instruction in Korean engineering education. *Korean Journal of Applied Linguistics*, *21*, 155–174.

Kaplan, H. (2018). Teachers' autonomy support, autonomy suppression, and conditional negative regard as predictors of optimal learning experience among high-achieving Bedouin students. *Social Psychology of Education*, *21*, 223–255. https://doi.org/10.1007/s11218-017-9405-y

Konno, K. (2011). Temporal shifts in L2 selves in the EFL classrooms. *Language Education & Technology*, *48*, 23–48.

Macaro, E. (2018). *English medium instruction*. Oxford University Press.

Maekawa, Y., & Yashima, T. (2012). Examining the motivational effect of presentation-based instruction on Japanese engineering students: From the viewpoints of the ideal self and self-determination theory. *Language Education & Technology*, *49*, 65–92. https://doi.org/10.24539/let.49.0_65

Malcolm, D. (2013). Motivational challenges for Gulf Arab students studying medicine in English. In E. Ushioda (Ed.), *International perspectives on motivation: Language learning and professional challenges* (pp. 98–116). Palgrave Macmillan. https://doi.org/10.1057/9781137000873_6

Markus, H., & Nurius, P. (1986). Possible selves. *American Psychologist*, *41*(9), 954–969. https://doi.org/10.1037/0003-066x.41.9.954

Ministry of Education, Culture, Sports, Science and Technology (MEXT). (2019). *Heisei 28 nenndo no daigaku ni okeru kyouikunaiyounado no kaikakujyoukyou ni tsuite* [The current situation of educational reform at universities in 2016]. https://www.mext.go.jp/a_menu/koutou/daigaku/04052801/__icsFiles/afieldfile/2019/05/28/1417336_001.pdf

Niemiec, C. P., & Ryan, R. M. (2009). Autonomy, competence, and relatedness in the classroom: Applying self-determination theory to educational practice. *Theory and Research in Education, 7*(2), 133–144. https://doi.org/10.1177/1477878509104318

Nishida, R. (2013). The L2 self, motivation, international posture, willingness to communicate and can-do among Japanese university learners of English. *Language Education & Technology, 50,* 43–67. https://doi.org/10.24539/let.50.0_43

Noels, K. A. (2001). Learning Spanish as a second language: Learners' orientations and perceptions of their teachers' communication style. *Language Learning, 51*(1), 107–144. https://doi.org/10.1111/0023-8333.00149

Noels, K. A., Clément, R., & Pelletier, L. G. (1999). Perceptions of teachers' communicative style and students' intrinsic and extrinsic motivation. *The Modern Language Journal, 83*(1), 23–34. https://doi.org/10.1111/0026-7902.00003

Noels, K. A., Pelletier, L. G., Clément, R., & Vallerand, R. J. (2000). Why are you learning a second language? Motivational orientations and self-determination theory. *Language Learning, 50*(1), 57–85. https://doi.org/10.1111/0023-8333.00111

Pulcini, V., & Campagna, S. (2015). Internationalization and the EMI controversy in Italian higher education. In S. Dimova, A. K. Hultgren, & C. Jensen (Eds.), *English-medium instruction in European higher education* (pp. 65–88). De Gruyter Mouton. https://doi.org/10.1515/9781614515272-005

Rawsthorne, L. J., & Elliot, A. J. (1999). Achievement goals and intrinsic motivation: A meta-analytic review. *Personality and Social Psychology Review, 3*(4), 326–344. https://doi.org/10.1207/s15327957pspr0304_3

Reeve, J. (2002). Self-determination theory applied to educational settings. In E. L. Deci & R. M. Ryan (Eds.), *Handbook of self-determination research* (pp. 183–203). University of Rochester Press.

Ryan, S. (2009). Self and identity in L2 motivation in Japan: The ideal L2 self and Japanese learners of English. In Z. Dörnyei & E. Ushioda (Eds.), *Motivation, language identity and the L2 self* (pp. 120–143). Multilingual Matters. https://doi.org/10.21832/9781847691293-007

Ryan, R. M., & Deci, E. L. (2000). Self-determination theory and the facilitation of intrinsic motivation, social development, and well-being. *American Psychologist, 55*(1), 68–78. https://doi.org/10.1037/0003-066x.55.1.68

Ryan, R. M., & Deci, E. L. (2002). An overview of self-determination theory: An organismic-dialectical perspective. In E. L. Deci & R. M. Ryan (Eds.), *Handbook of self-determination research* (pp. 3–33). University of Rochester Press.

Schmidt-Unterberger, B. (2018). The English-medium paradigm: a conceptualization of English-medium teaching in higher education. *International Journal of Bilingual Education and Bilingualism, 21,* 527–539. https://doi.org/10.1080/13670050.2018.1491949

Sert, N. (2008). The language of instruction dilemma in the Turkish context. *System, 36*(2), 156–171. https://doi.org/10.1016/j.system.2007.11.006

Shimauchi, S. (2016). *Higashi Ajia ni okeru ryugakusei ido no paradaimu tenkan: Daigaku kokusaika to 'Eigo puroguramu' no hikkan hikaku* [Paradigm shift on international student mobility in East Asia: Comparative analysis on internationalization of higher education and English-medium degree programs in Japan and South Korea]. Toshindo.

Shimauchi, S. (2018). Gender in English-medium instruction programs: Differences in international awareness? In A. Bradford & H. Brown (Eds.), *English-medium instruction in Japanese higher education: Policy, challenges and outcomes* (pp. 180–194). Multilingual Matters. https://doi.org/10.21832/9781783098958-014

Skinner, E., & Edge, K. (2002). Self-determination, coping, and development. In E. L. Deci & R. M. Ryan (Eds.), *Handbook of self-determination research* (pp. 297–337). University of Rochester Press.

Taguchi, T., Magid, M., & Papi, M. (2009). The L2 motivational self system among Japanese, Chinese and Iranian learners of English: A comparative study. In Z. Dörnyei & E. Ushioda (Eds.), *Motivation, language identity and the L2 self* (pp. 66–97). Multilingual Matters. https://doi.org/10.21832/9781847691293-005

Tanaka, H., & Hiromori, T. (2007). The effects of educational intervention that enhances intrinsic motivation of L2 students. *JALT Journal, 29*(1), 59–80. https://doi.org/10.37546/JALTJJ29.1-3

Tsuneyoshi, R. (2005). Internationalization strategies in Japan: The dilemmas and possibilities of study abroad programs using English. *Journal of Research in International Education, 4*(1), 65–86. https://doi.org/10.1177/1475240905050291

Turhan, B., & Kirkgöz, Y. (2018). Motivation of engineering students and lecturers toward English medium instruction at tertiary level in Turkey. *Journal of Language and Linguistic Studies, 14*(1), 261–277. https://www.jlls.org/index.php/jlls/article/view/842/356

Wilkinson, R. (2005). *The impact of language on teaching content: Views from the content teacher.* Retrieved 21 December 2011 http://www. palmenia. helsinki.fi/congress/bilingual2005 presentations/wilkinson.pdf

Wilkinson, R. (2011). If all business education were in English, would it matter? *ITL – International Journal of Applied Linguistics, 161*, 111–123. https//doi.org/10.1075/itl.161.07wil

Wu, W. (2006). Students' attitudes toward EMI: Using Chung Hua University as an example. *Journal of Education and Foreign Language and Literature, 4*, 67–84.

Yashima, T. (2009). International posture and the ideal L2 self in the Japanese EFL context. In Z. Dörnyei & E. Ushioda (Eds.), *Motivation, language identity and the L2 self* (pp. 144–163). Multilingual Matters. https://doi.org/10.21832/9781847691293-008

Yashima, T., Nishida, R., & Mizumoto, A. (2017). Influence of learner beliefs and gender on the motivating power of L2 selves. *The Modern Language Journal, 101*(4), 691–711. https://doi.org/10.1111/modl.12430

Yashima, T., Noels, K., Shizuka, T., Takeuchi, O., Yamane, S., & Yoshizawa, K. (2009). The interplay of classroom anxiety, intrinsic motivation, and gender in the Japanese EFL context. *Kansai University Journal of Foreign Language Education and Research*, *17*, 41–64.

Yonezawa, A. (2011). The internationalization of Japanese higher education: Policy debates and realities. In S. Marginson, S. Kaur, & E. Sawir (Eds.), *Higher education in the Asia-Pacific: Strategic responses to globalization* (pp. 329–342). Springer. https://doi.org/10.1007/978-94-007-1500-4

# 3 Two faces of EMI motivation
## Learning English and content

## Study 1: A quantitative study to uncover what EMI motivation is

In theory, English-medium instruction (EMI) is for content learning but not for language learning. However, previous research conducted in Japanese universities (Chapple, 2015; Shimauchi, 2018) and the small-scale survey and interview project discussed in Chapter 2 imply that EMI motivation could be composed of motivation to learn English and content. Therefore, to explore what EMI motivation is in depth, I conducted a new, larger quantitative study (Study 1) by applying self-determination theory (SDT) as the principal framework. This chapter discusses Study 1, aiming to identify the factors that influence EMI intrinsic motivation and EMI identified regulation (RQs 1 & 2) as well as groups of students with different motivational profiles (RQ 3). The study also reveals how students perform differently when their profile differs. The research questions are follows:

(1) Which factors influence students' highly self-determined types of motivation, namely, EMI intrinsic motivation and EMI identified regulation?
(2) Which psychological needs in the framework of SDT should be satisfied for EMI intrinsic motivation to be enhanced?
(3) Are there different motivational profiles among the students? If so, how are they different?

### *Method*

Two hundred and twenty-one Japanese students (138 females, 80 males, and three unknown) majoring in social studies or management responded to a survey about EMI motivation, motivation to learn

English and content. Year groups of the participants varied: 16 were freshmen, 59 were sophomores, 75 were juniors, 60 were seniors, and 6 were in their fifth year of university. The mean of their self-reported TOEFL ITP scores was 474.59 ($SD = 42.15$), with 600 being the highest and 310 the lowest.

A survey was administered between late April and early July 2015 to students in nine courses taught by seven EMI disciplinary instructors. The survey was administered halfway through the course, either during or after class. Due to the semester and quarter systems employed by the university, the timing of the survey varied. Students in four courses completed the survey between late April and early May in the first quarter. In one course, the survey was carried out in late May in the spring semester and, in the remaining four courses, it was conducted between late June and early July in the second quarter.

The course content also varied, including topics such as cultural studies, international sociology, international relations (four different courses in the same discipline), international issues and policy, Japanese culture and society, media and culture, and communication studies. All courses in this study were presented in the form of lectures, with a maximum class size of 250 students. Some classes had more than two hundred students, while others only had approximately fifty students. I observed the classes when I administered the survey and noticed that some courses had relatively small numbers of students, but the pedagogical approach in each class was quite similar. In other words, all the classes observed were taught in the one-way lecture style. Hence, students' answers would be only minimally affected by the class size. All the class materials were written, and lectures were conducted in English. In terms of reading assignments, some used articles and/or book chapters in English, while others tried to cover an entire book during the course.

For the present study, the survey consisted of 81 questions, and several survey measures were either adopted or adapted from previous research. Most of the survey items related to motivation were rated using six-point Likert scales, which followed the previous research conducted by Ryan (2009) and Yashima et al. (2009). In addition, a percentage of self-reported understanding of the EMI lectures, minutes of average weekly self-study time for the relevant EMI course, and self-reported TOEFL ITP scores were recorded.

To assess student intrinsic motivation, extrinsic motivation, and amotivation in EMI, the translated version of the survey instrument employed by Noels et al. (2000), which has been used in the studies conducted by Hiromori and Tanaka (2006) and Yashima et al. (2009), was applied. Since the items in their studies were designed to explore motivation in language classrooms, minor changes were made to adapt them to the EMI context (e.g., "English" was replaced with "EMI"). Integrated regulation was not included in the survey because it was difficult to distinguish from identified regulation for university students as they could be too young to have developed an integrated sense of self in school (Noels et al., 2000; Vallerand et al., 1989).

To assess the level of self-regulation in EMI, three items (Cronbach's $\alpha = .81$) served to evaluate amotivation (e.g., "I don't understand why I have to study EMI"); two items ($r = .56$) were used to measure intrinsic motivation (e.g., "EMI is exciting"); two items ($r = .65$) were utilized to measure external regulation (e.g., "I am taking EMI because I want to get enough credits to graduate"); and three items (Cronbach's $\alpha = .80$) were adapted for identified regulation (e.g., "I want to acquire disciplinary knowledge in English for use in the future"). Items that attempted to assess introjected regulation were deleted because of low reliability (Cronbach's $\alpha = .45$).

Three items in each subscale served to evaluate the degree of satisfaction of the three psychological needs within SDT that influence intrinsic motivation (i.e., the need for autonomy, competence, and relatedness). Three items (Cronbach's $\alpha = .76$) were used to measure fulfillment of the need for autonomy (e.g., "Teachers in EMI ask for the students' opinions about the content and/or procedure of the class"); three items (Cronbach's $\alpha = .70$) assessed fulfillment of the need for competence (e.g., "I feel a sense of accomplishment in EMI"); and three items (Cronbach's $\alpha = .75$) assessed satisfaction of the need for relatedness (e.g., "I get along with my classmates in EMI").

Regarding the variables related to motivation to learn English, motivational intensity (intended effort) to learn English was measured via six items (Cronbach's $\alpha = .79$) adopted from Ryan (2008) and Yashima (2002) (e.g., "If English were not taught in school, I would try to go to English classes somewhere else"). Further, four items (Cronbach's $\alpha = .80$) reflected participants' attitudes to learning English (e.g., "I really enjoy learning English"). These items were adopted from Ryan (2008).

Finally, regarding the items based on the L2 motivational self system, six items (Cronbach's $\alpha = .85$) were taken from Ryan (2008) to assess ideal L2 self, which is how vividly a participant could visualize their future ideal self as an English speaker (e.g., "I often imagine myself as someone who is able to speak English"). Further, another four items (Cronbach's $\alpha = .64$) were taken from Ryan (2008) to evaluate participants' ought-to L2 self, which is their image of what they should become (e.g., "Hardly anybody really cares whether I learn English or not").

Regarding the variables related to motivation to learn content, motivational intensity (intended effort) to learn content was measured with six items (Cronbach's α = .79). These items were adapted from the items that Ryan (2008) and Yashima (2002) used to assess intended effort to learn English. For example, "English" was replaced with "this subject," as in "I often think about this subject or the content that I learned from this class."

Finally, two items ($r = .47$) were employed to evaluate participants' background knowledge concerning the content they were studying when the survey was conducted. These items were created based on the results of the first small-scale study discussed in Chapter 2 (e.g., "I already had a lot of knowledge related to this subject before taking this course"). Pilot surveys were administered to five participants and subsequently revised according to their feedback.

Students' average weekly self-study time for the relevant EMI course and self-reported understanding of the EMI lectures, and TOEFL ITP scores were also recorded. These were added as a result of the findings of the small study, which highlighted the possible effect of students' poor understanding of EMI lectures on student motivation.

## Results

Before analyzing the data, Kolmogorov-Smirnov tests were performed to examine the normality of the data (Table 3.1). The tests revealed that the data for intended effort to learn English, attitude to learning English, intended effort to learn content, and TOEFL ITP score were normally distributed. However, the other factors such as the ideal L2 self, the ought-to L2 self, EMI amotivation, external regulation, identified regulation, intrinsic motivation, the need for autonomy, the need for competence, the need for relatedness, and self-evaluation of background knowledge were not. Additionally, their self-reported understanding of EMI lectures and weekly self-study time were not normally distributed either. Although some of the data were not normally distributed, with large sample sizes of over thirty, violation of normal distribution does not usually cause significant problems[1] (see Pallant, 2001).

Descriptive statistics and correlation analyses were conducted to investigate the potential relationships between various factors in this study, as well as to confirm the results of the previous research in language classrooms (Ryan, 2009; Taguchi et al., 2009) (see Tables 3.1, 3.2, and 3.3). As indicated in Table 3.2, the motivational variables for

*Table 3.1* Descriptive statistics for each variable in Study 1

| Variable | | Mean | SD | Sig Kolmogorov-Smirnov test | Skewness | Kurtosis |
|---|---|---|---|---|---|---|
| Motivational regulations for EMI | Amotivation | 2.56 | 1.16 | .002 | .60 | .36 |
| | External regulation | 4.10 | 1.43 | .000 | -.39 | -.61 |
| | Identified regulation | 4.09 | 1.23 | .001 | -.47 | .05 |
| | Intrinsic motivation | 3.79 | 1.26 | .000 | -.05 | -.36 |
| The three psychological needs[a] | Need for autonomy | 3.36 | 1.13 | .005 | -.08 | -.38 |
| | Need for competence | 3.21 | 1.04 | .012 | .07 | -.337 |
| | Need for relatedness | 3.96 | 1.08 | .000 | -.10 | -.54 |
| | Intended effort to learn English | 4.02 | .89 | .200 | -.02 | -.21 |
| Motivational variables for learning English | Attitude to learning English | 4.34 | 1.00 | .095 | -.31 | -.14 |
| | Ideal L2 self | 4.54 | 1.05 | .006 | -.76 | .34 |
| | Ought-to L2 self | 4.41 | .96 | .000 | -.70 | .46 |
| Motivational variable for learning content | Intended effort to learn content | 3.14 | 1.06 | .054 | .13 | -.40 |
| Self-evaluation of background knowledge | | 2.36 | 1.06 | .000 | .30 | -.67 |
| Understanding of the lectures[b] (%) | | 52.27 | 20.10 | .000 | -.23 | -.74 |
| Weekly self-study time (min) | | 88.40 | 111.63 | .000 | 4.53 | 27.63 |
| TOEFL ITP | | 475.70 | 3.54 | .200 | -.29 | .84 |

Notes:
[a] Represents the fulfillment of the three psychological needs within SDT.
[b] Represents participants' self-perception of their understanding of the lectures.

*Table 3.2* Correlations between motivational variables for learning English, motivational variables for learning content, and self–evaluation of background knowledge

| Variable | | Intended effort to learn English | Attitude to learning English | Ideal L2 self | Ought-to L2 self | Intended effort to learn content |
|---|---|---|---|---|---|---|
| Motivational variables for learning English | Intended effort to learn English | | | | | |
| | Attitude to learning English | .72** | | | | |
| | Ideal L2 self | .68** | .64** | | | |
| | Ought-to L2 self | .30** | .35** | .54** | | |
| Motivational variables for learning content | Intended effort to learn content | .37** | .23** | .27** | .10 | −.01 |
| Self-evaluation of background knowledge | | .13 | −.04 | .02 | −.13 | .39** |

Note: **$p < .01$.

learning English (i.e., intended effort to learn English, the ideal L2 self, the ought-to L2 self, and attitude to learning English) correlated either highly positively or positively with each other. A positive correlation was also found between intended effort to learn English and to learn the content of the respective course ($r = .37$, $p < .001$), although the association was not strong. Moreover, positive correlations were revealed between intended effort to learn the content and self-evaluation of background knowledge ($r = .39$, $p < .001$). Regarding the correlation between intended effort to learn English and EMI motivation (e.g., EMI intrinsic motivation, EMI identified regulation), Table 3.3 shows that intended effort to learn English correlated positively with EMI intrinsic motivation ($r = .53$, $p < .001$) and EMI identified regulation ($r = .53$, $p < .001$). The ideal L2 self also correlated positively with EMI intrinsic motivation ($r = .56$, $p < .001$), and strongly correlated positively with EMI identified regulation ($r = .69$, $p < .001$). Finally, attitude to learning English correlated positively with EMI intrinsic motivation ($r = .54$, $p < .001$). Regarding the three psychological needs within the framework of SDT, the needs for autonomy, competence, and relatedness are all either positively correlated or strongly positively correlated (see Table 3.4). To illustrate, the positive correlations between the need for autonomy and the need for competence ($r = .64$, $p < .001$) as well as the need for autonomy and the need for relatedness are strong ($r = .67$, $p < .001$). In addition, the need for competence and the need for relatedness are positively correlated ($r = .53$, $p < .001$). Those results are in line with Ryan and Deci's (2000) suggestion that the three psychological needs are all interrelated and, therefore, they are all necessary, and one cannot replace another as other previous studies presented (Hiromori, 2005; Hiromori & Tanaka, 2006).

To answer RQ1 (i.e., Which factors influence students' highly self-determined types of motivation, namely, EMI intrinsic motivation and EMI identified regulation?), two stepwise multiple regression analyses were conducted[2] (see Tables 3.5 and 3.6).

In the first analysis, the dependent variable was EMI intrinsic motivation, and the independent variables were intended effort to learn English, the ideal L2 self, the ought-to L2 self, attitude to learning English, TOEFL ITP score, intended effort to learn content, participants' self-reporting of their understanding of the EMI lectures, and average weekly self-study time. In the second analysis, the dependent variable was EMI identified regulation, and the independent variables were the same as for the first analysis. The regression model for predictors for EMI intrinsic motivation was significant ($F$ [3,177] = 40.46, $p < .001$,

*Table 3.3* Correlations between motivational regulations of EMI, motivational variables for learning English, and motivational variables for learning content

| Variable | | Motivational regulations of EMI | | | |
| --- | --- | --- | --- | --- | --- |
| | | *Intrinsic motivation* | *Identified regulation* | *External regulation* | *Amotivation* |
| Motivational variables for learning English | Intended effort to learn English | .53** | .53** | −.24** | −.39** |
| | Attitude to learning English | .54** | .49** | −.25** | −.30** |
| | Ideal L2 self | .56** | .69** | −.20** | −.33** |
| | Ought-to L2 self | .30** | .41** | .01 | −.05 |
| Motivational variables for learning content | Intended effort to learn content | .39** | .38** | −.12 | −.15* |
| Self- evaluation of background knowledge | | .11 | .05 | −.04 | .20** |

Note: $^*p < .05$, $^{**}p < .01$.

*Table 3.4* Correlations between the three psychological needs within the framework of SDT

| Variable | Need for autonomy | Need for competence |
|---|---|---|
| Need for competence | .64** | |
| Need for relatedness | .67** | .53** |

Note: **$p < .01$.

*Table 3.5* Results of multiple regression analysis predicting EMI intrinsic motivation

| Variable | B | SE B | β |
|---|---|---|---|
| Attitude to learning English | .39 | .09 | .31*** |
| Ideal L2 self | .36 | .09 | .30*** |
| Intended effort to learn content | .26 | .07 | .22*** |

Notes:
$R^2 = .41$***
*** $p < .001$.

*Table 3.6* Results of multiple regression analysis predicting EMI identified regulation

| Variable | B | SE B | β |
|---|---|---|---|
| Ideal L2 self | .74 | .06 | .63*** |
| Intended effort to learn content | .25 | .06 | .22*** |

Notes:
$R^2 = .52$***
*** $p < .001$.

$\eta^2 = .41$). The three significant predictors of EMI intrinsic motivation were as follows: attitude to learning English, $\beta = .31$ ($p < .001$), ideal L2 self, $\beta = .30$ ($p < .001$), and intended effort to learn content, $\beta = .22$ ($p < .001$). Variation inflation factors (VIF) were assessed to detect multicollinearity, and no problem was found. The scores were as follows: attitude to learning English, 1.58, ideal L2 self, 1.63, and intended effort to learn content, 1.08.[3]

Another regulation model to identify the predictors of EMI identified regulation was significant as well ($F$ [2, 179] = 94.51, $p < .001$,

$\eta^2 = .52$). The results indicated that the ideal L2 self ($\beta = .63$, $p < .001$) and intended effort to learn content ($\beta = .22$, $p < .001$) influence EMI identified regulation. The VIFs once again showed no problem of multicollinearity. The scores for the ideal L2 self and intended effort to learn content were both 1.08. For both EMI intrinsic motivation and EMI identified regulation, variables related to learning English are more influential than intended effort to learn content. Among the variables of motivation to learn English, ideal L2 self is an influential factor for both EMI intrinsic motivation and EMI identified regulation, although for enhancing EMI intrinsic motivation, attitude to learning English is more critical.

Two multiple regression analyses were conducted to answer RQ2 (i.e., Which psychological needs in the framework of SDT should be satisfied for intrinsic motivation to be enhanced?) (see Table 3.7). The results showed that the need for competence is a predictor of EMI intrinsic motivation ($F$ [1, 210] = 84.94, $p < .001$, $\eta^2 =. 29$). The VIF score for the need for competence was 1.00, indicating no problem of multicollinearity. Another multiple regression analysis was conducted to identify the predictors of EMI identified regulation within the framework of SDT (see Table 3.8). The results demonstrated that the degrees of satisfaction of the needs for competence and relatedness affected EMI identified regulation ($F$ [1, 210] =30.25, $p < .001$, $\eta^2 =. 29$). The

*Table 3.7* Results of multiple regression analysis predicting EMI intrinsic motivation

| Variable | B | SE B | $\beta$ |
|---|---|---|---|
| Need for competence | .66 | .07 | .54*** |

Notes:
$R^2= .29$***
*** $p < .001$.

*Table 3.8* Results of multiple regression analysis predicting EMI identified regulation

| Variable | B | SE B | $\beta$ |
|---|---|---|---|
| Need for competence | .43 | .08 | .36*** |
| Need for relatedness | .19 | .08 | .17* |

Notes:
$R^2= .22$**
* $p < .05$, ** $p < .01$, ***$p < .001$.

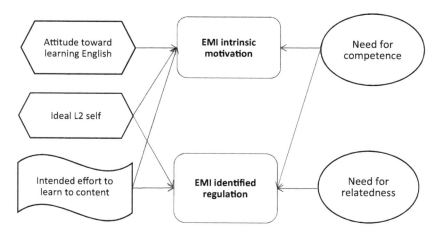

*Figure 3.1* Summary of regression analyses.

VIF scores for both the needs for competence and relatedness were 1.40, indicating no problem of multicollinearity. The results responding to RQs 1 and 2 are summarized in Figure 3.1. Fulfilling the need for competence has a direct influence on maintaining or enhancing EMI intrinsic motivation and identified regulation. For EMI identified regulation, in addition to fulfillment of the need for competence, satisfaction of the need for relatedness is significantly important.

A hierarchical cluster analysis was employed to answer RQ3 (i.e., Are there different motivational profiles among the students? If so, how are they different?). The analysis was implemented based on two factors: intended effort to learn English and intended effort to learn content. Hierarchical clustering was applied using Euclidean distance. A dendrogram indicating the hierarchical clustering structure was used to determine cutoff points. Three clusters were subsequently identified: Cluster 1 characterizing average motivation (119 participants), Cluster 2 characterizing low motivation (58 participants), and Cluster 3 characterizing high motivation (44 participants). An analysis of variance (ANOVA) confirmed significant differences in intended effort to learn English and intended effort to learn content between the clusters. The ANOVA was also used to identify statistical differences between the clusters (see Table 3.9 and Figures 3.2 and 3.3). As shown in Table 3.9, significant differences were found, particularly for EMI intrinsic motivation ($F$ [2, 216] = 15.36, $p < .001$, $\eta^2 = .13$), the need for competence ($F$ [2, 214] = 18.18, $p < .001$, $\eta^2 = .05$), the need for autonomy ($F$

*Table 3.9* Comparisons of descriptive statistics for intrinsic/extrinsic motivation and psychological factors among the cluster

| Variable | | Cluster 1 Average motivation | | Cluster 2 Low motivation | | Cluster 3 High motivation | | Post-hoc (Tukey) |
|---|---|---|---|---|---|---|---|---|
| | | Mean | SD | Mean | SD | Mean | SD | |
| Motivational variables for learning English | Intended effort to learn English | 3.99 | .76 | 3.59 | .97 | 4.69 | .73 | 1 > 2, 1 < 3, 2 < 3 |
| | Attitude to learning English | 4.38 | .87 | 3.98 | 1.14 | 4.70 | .98 | 1 > 2, 2 < 3 |
| | Ideal L2 self | 4.67 | .88 | 4.03 | 1.22 | 4.87 | 1.04 | 1 > 2, 2 < 3 |
| | Ought-to L2 self | 4.47 | .85 | 4.19 | 1.09 | 4.54 | 1.02 | ns |
| Motivational variable for learning content | Intended effort to learn content | 3.22 | .46 | 1.85 | .46 | 4.65 | .56 | 1 > 2, 1 < 3, 2 < 3 |
| Motivational regulations for EMI | Amotivation | 2.52 | 1.00 | 2.82 | 1.30 | 2.31 | 1.35 | ns |
| | External regulation | 4.23 | 1.29 | 4.10 | 1.45 | 3.80 | 1.70 | ns |
| | Identified regulation | 4.21 | .92 | 3.40 | 1.51 | 4.69 | 1.13 | 1 > 2, 2 < 3 |
| | Intrinsic motivation | 3.80 | 1.10 | 3.20 | 1.35 | 4.52 | 1.21 | 1 > 2, 1 < 3, 2 < 3 |
| Three psychological needs[a] | Need for competence | 3.31 | .88 | 2.60 | 1.05 | 3.74 | 1.07 | 1 > 2, 1 < 3, 2 < 3 |
| | Need for autonomy | 3.38 | .95 | 2.86 | 1.19 | 3.98 | 1.18 | 1 > 2, 1 < 3, 2 < 3 |
| | Need for relatedness | 3.95 | .91 | 3.67 | 1.27 | 4.36 | 1.13 | 2 < 3 |

Notes:
Comparisons of descriptive statistics for intrinsic/extrinsic motivation and psychological factors among the cluster.
[a] Represents the fulfillment of the three psychological needs within the framework of SDT.

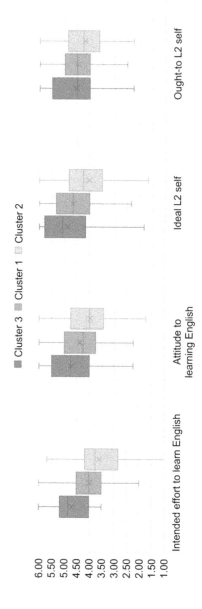

*Figure 3.2* Motivational variables for learning English for each cluster.

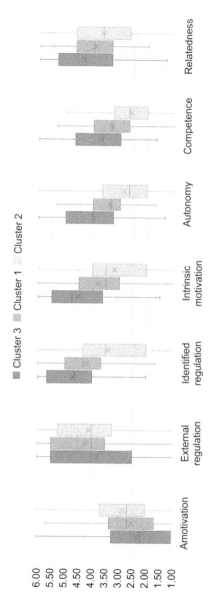

*Figure 3.3* EMI motivational profiles for each cluster.

*Table 3.10* Descriptive statistics for self-reported understanding of the EMI lectures and self–study time for each cluster

| Variable | Cluster 1 Average motivation | | Cluster 2 Low motivation | | Cluster 3 High motivation | | Post-hoc (Tukey) |
|---|---|---|---|---|---|---|---|
| | Mean | SD | Mean | SD | Mean | SD | |
| Understanding of the lectures[a] (%) | 51.92 | 19.91 | 48.6 | 20.31 | 63.21 | 17.17 | 1< 3, 2 < 3 |
| Weekly self-study time (min) | 77.28 | 74.46 | 51.89 | 55.75 | 163.72 | 188.71 | 1 < 3, 2 < 3 |
| TOEFL ITP | 471 | 40.65 | 470 | 42.52 | 489 | 43.55 | ns |

Note:
[a] Represents participants' self-perception of their understanding of the lectures.

[2, 214] = 13.55, $p < .001$, $\eta^2 = .11$), and self-evaluation of background knowledge ($F[2, 218] = 13.10, p < .001, \eta^2 = .11$).

Statistical differences between Cluster 3 (see Figure 3.2), the group with the highest motivation, and Cluster 2, the group with the lowest motivation, were found for attitude to learning English ($F[2, 218] = 7.24, p < .01, \eta^2 = .06$), the ideal L2 self ($F[2, 214] = 10.48, p < .001, \eta^2 = .09$), EMI identified regulation ($F[2, 217] = 17.39, p < .001, \eta^2 = .14$), and the need for relatedness ($F[2, 217] = 5.21, p < .01, \eta^2 = .05$) (see Table 3.9 and Figures 3.2 and 3.3).

Furthermore, as Table 3.10 and Figure 3.4 show, significant differences were revealed among the clusters for participants' self-reported understanding of the EMI lectures ($F[2, 208] = 7.36, p < .01, \eta^2 = .07$) and weekly self-study time for EMI ($F[2, 208] = 15.01, p < 001, \eta^2 = .13$). Considering the data in Tables 3.9 and 3.10, as well as in Figures 3.2 and 3.3, the results of the cluster analysis are in line with Vallerand and Bissonnette (1992), who demonstrated that self-determined types of extrinsic motivation (such as identified regulation) correlate positively with persistent behavior. However, there was no significant difference in TOEFL ITP scores among the three clusters (Table 3.10).

The results suggest that students who are more motivated try harder and understand the lectures more. It means that what they bring to the classroom (i.e., English proficiency) does not determine how hard they try or how competent they feel, but that students who are more motivated in EMI classrooms try their best to understand the lectures regardless of their English proficiency.

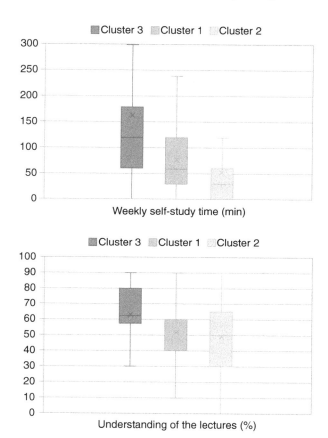

*Figure 3.4* Self-reported understanding of the EMI lectures and self-study time for each cluster.

## *Discussion*

Regarding RQ1, as indicated by the first small-scale study introduced in Chapter 2, EMI intrinsic motivation and EMI identified regulation is a combination of the students' drive to learn English and content. Shimauchi (2018) and Chapple (2015) explored why Japanese students take EMI and found that they value improving their English proficiency more than gaining content knowledge through EMI. Study 1, which applied SDT as a theoretical framework and focused on different dimensions of motivation (i.e., what EMI motivation is and what maintains EMI motivation), added that students' positive attitudes to learning English and the vividness of their images of their ideal selves as English speakers are stronger motivators than their intended effort to learn content. Further, students can internalize the significance of opting for EMI when they know what kind of English speaker they want to become. In fact, studies in English language classrooms have reported that visualizing their ideal L2 self can enhance their intended effort to learn English, which will eventually help improve their English proficiency (Dörnyei, 2009; Ryan, 2009; Taguchi et al., 2009). In other words, this study confirmed that EMI classrooms are not separate from English language classrooms but rather part of a continuum from the student's perspective, as Macaro (2018) proposed.

The results obtained in answering RQ2 revealed that students enjoy EMI more when they feel competent and have a sense of self-efficacy. Moreover, they may find taking EMI is personally beneficial when they have a trustworthy relationship with their peers and teachers in addition to feeling competent. These results are partially in line with Hiromori's (2005) study in a Japanese university, which reports that the need for competence and autonomy directly influenced students' engagement in language classrooms. In his study, the impact of the degree of satisfaction of the need for relatedness was statistically significant to intrinsic motivation in addition to identified regulation. He suggested that it could be so because the need for competence and relatedness absorb the component of the need for autonomy and represent its influence on intrinsic motivation and identified regulation. Although the results are not the same as his study, this was also observed in the current study as the results showed a strong positive correlation between the three psychological needs (see Table 3.4).

Further, the results of the regression analyses in the current study do not mean that the need for autonomy is not necessary in EMI contexts. In fact, Hiromori and Tanaka (2006) conducted an interventional study in an English language classrooms in a Japanese University and revealed that the needs for autonomy and competence have a bigger impact on the enhancement of intrinsic motivation to learn English than the need for relatedness has. Moreover, Ryan and Deci (2000) stated that the three psychological needs are all necessary, but how essential they are, depends on the context.

Finally, with regard to the results of the analysis to respond to RQ3, there is a group of students who are motivated and not in EMI classrooms. Comparing them with the aim to reveal the differences between the group with high motivation and the group with low motivation indicated that students who are motivated devote more time to studying for EMI and consequently understand the lectures better. This means that when the pedagogical approaches can enhance students' EMI intrinsic motivation and EMI identified regulation, the students will study more and comprehend more, which as a consequence will lead to higher motivation.

**The significance of motivation to learn English, the need for competence and relatedness**

The larger quantitative study discussed in this chapter showed that, in reality, motivation to learn English has a significant role in EMI classrooms. The results were interesting in two aspects: what motivates students to choose EMI classes, and what motivates their performance in those classes. First, students' motivation to opt for EMI classes is related to language learning, especially positive attitudes to learning English, and their desire to minimize the gap between their present self and ideal self as English speakers, and their drive to gain knowledge of the content—these comprise EMI motivation. Contrary to the definition of EMI in theory, that EMI is for content learning, and therefore language learning need not be a part of the agenda, student motivation related to language learning has a more influential role than that of motivation to learning content. Also, in terms of students' performance in EMI classes, from the perspective of SDT, the study revealed that students feeling a sense of growth and achievement is important to motivate them internally. In addition to the sense of achievement, a sense of belonging is important to internalize their value of opting for EMI.

Finally, the study revealed that students with high motivation better understand the lectures and exert more effort to study in EMI. It means that the results suggested that highly motivated students are in a virtuous circle and that they can enjoy EMI because they put more effort into it. Successful learning experiences will boost their motivation further, which will lead to more motivated behaviors. On the other hand, students with low motivation are in a vicious circle. Therefore, if EMI is taught in an accessible way for Japanese students, they will be motivated and study harder, which will further increase their comprehension of lectures.

Study 1 in this chapter identified factors that are important in an EMI context. Yet, whether or not students' needs for autonomy, competence, and relatedness are fulfilled, remains unknown. Accordingly, the next chapter will discuss Study 2, a qualitative study that addresses these questions.

# Notes

1  Participants' self-reported understanding of the EMI lectures and average weekly self-study time were not normally distributed, regardless of the sample size. Therefore, I refer to the results of these factors in this study to gain a deeper understanding of students' motivation in EMI. Regarding other psychological factors in the survey, I checked if the factors had a bell-shaped distribution with histograms; to some degree, they did. In addition, the factors in this study have been widely employed in many empirical studies in language classrooms (e.g., Hiromori, 2006; Maekawa & Yashima, 2012; Ryan, 2008; Yashima et al., 2009). In those studies, parametric tests were used. Thus, the reliability of the items in this current study should also be sufficient to conduct parametric tests. With regard to multiple regression analyses, the results were considered not to be strongly influenced by a violation of normal distribution in this type of case (i.e., factors are assumed for normal distribution to some extent based on the histograms), and non-parametric tests were not recommended (Mizumoto, personal communication, March 6, 2019; see also https:// stats.stackexchange.com/questions/268213/non-parametric-alternative-to- multiple-linear-regression for a reference). For these reasons, parametric tests were applied in the current study.

2  Multiple regression analyses assume that when one factor moves, another one is not going to move. In other words, the analysis has a premise that there is no correlation at all among the factors. However, there are correlations among factors to some degree in an empirical study, including this one.

3  The VIF were low enough to perform a multiple regression analysis, although there are some interrelations between the three psychological needs.

# References

Chapple, J. (2015). Teaching in English is not necessarily the teaching of English. *International Education Studies, 8*(3), 1–13. https://doi.org/10.5539/ ies.v8n3p1

Dörnyei, Z. (2009). The L2 motivational self system. In Z. Dörnyei & E. Ushioda (Eds.), *Motivation, language identity and the L2 self* (pp. 9–42). Multilingual Matters. https://doi.org/10.21832/9781847691293-003

Hiromori, T. (2005). Three factors that motivate L2 learners: From the perspectives of general tendency and individual differences. *JACET Bulletin, 41*, 37–50.

Hiromori, T. (2006). The effects of educational intervention on L2 learners' motivational development. *JACET Bulletin, 43*, 1–14.

Hiromori, T., & Tanaka, H. (2006). Instructional intervention on motivating English learners: The self-determination theory viewpoint. *Language Education and Technology, 43,* 111–126.

Macaro, E. (2018). *English medium instruction*. Oxford University Press.

Maekawa, Y., & Yashima, T. (2012). Examining the motivational effect of presentation-based instruction on Japanese engineering students: From the viewpoints of the ideal self and self-determination theory. *Language Education & Technology, 49*, 65–92.

Noels, K. A., Pelletier, L. G., Clément, R., & Vallerand R. J. (2000). Why are you learning a second language? Motivational orientations and self-determination theory. *Language Learning, 50*, 57–85. https://doi.org/10.1111/0023-8333.00111

Pallant, J. (2001). *SPSS survival manual*. Open University Press.

Ryan, R. M., & Deci, E. L. (2000). Self-determination theory and the facilitation of intrinsic motivation, social development, and well-being. *American Psychologist, 55*(1), 68–78. https://doi.org/10.1037/0003-066x.55.1.68

Ryan, S. (2008). *The ideal L2 selves of Japanese learners of English* [Unpublished doctoral dissertation]. University of Nottingham. http://eprints.nottingham.ac.uk/10550/1/ryan-2008.pdf

Ryan, S. (2009). Self and identity in L2 motivation in Japan: The ideal L2 self and Japanese learners of English. In Z. Dörnyei & E. Ushioda (Eds.), *Motivation, language identity and the L2 self* (pp. 120–143). Multilingual Matters. https://doi.org/10.21832/9781847691293-007

Shimauchi, S. (2018). Gender in English-medium instruction programs: Differences in international awareness? In A. Bradford & H. Brown (Eds.), *English-medium instruction in Japanese higher education: Policy, challenges and outcomes* (pp. 180–194). Multilingual Matters. https://doi.org/10.21832/9781783098958-014

Taguchi, T., Magid, M., & Papi, M. (2009). The L2 motivational self system among Japanese, Chinese and Iranian learners of English: A comparative study. In Z. Dörnyei & E. Ushioda (Eds.), *Motivation, language identity and the L2 self* (pp. 66–97). Multilingual Matters. https://doi.org/10.21832/9781847691293-005

Vallerand, R. J., & Bissonnette, R. (1992). Intrinsic, extrinsic, and amotivational styles as predictors of behavior: A prospective study. *Journal of Personality. 60*, 599–620. https://doi.org/10.1111/j.1467-6494.1992.tb00922.x

Vallerand, R. J., Blais, M. R., Briére, N. M., & Pelletier, J. G. (1989). Construction et validation de l'Echelle de motivation en education (EME) [Construction and validation of the Motivation toward Education Scale]. *Canadian Journal of Behavioral Science / Revue canadienne des sciences du comportement, 21*(3), 323–349. https://doi.org/10.1037/h0079855

Yashima, T. (2002). Willingness to communicate in a second language: The Japanese EFL context. *The Modern Language Journal, 86*(1), 54–66. https://doi.org/10.1111/1540-4781.00136

Yashima, T., Noels, K., Shizuka, T., Takeuchi, O., Yamane, S., & Yoshizawa, K. (2009). The interplay of classroom anxiety, intrinsic motivation, and gender in the Japanese EFL context. *Kansai University Journal of Foreign Language Education and Research, 17*, 41–64

# 4 How do Japanese students feel in EMI classrooms?

The larger quantitative study to explore EMI motivation in depth in Chapter 3 (Study 1) confirmed that the fulfillment of the three psychological needs—the need for autonomy, competence, and relatedness—within self-determination theory (SDT) are essential to enhancing English-medium instruction (EMI) intrinsic motivation and identified regulation. Nevertheless, the degree of the fulfillment of the three psychological needs in actual EMI classrooms remains unknown. Therefore, I conducted a study to explore how students actually feel in EMI classrooms. The results identified some serious motivation issues in the University A EMI program and hinted at how the situation could be improved.

## Study 2: The need for autonomy, competence, and relatedness

### Method

Six participants who agreed to be interviewed during the larger-scale quantitative study discussed in Chapter 3 (Study 1) were also invited to participate in a qualitative follow-up study (hereafter Study 2). Based on the results of Study 1, two participants from each motivational group (high, average, and low) were interviewed. Some of the demographic information that was collected in Study 1 is also important for this current qualitative study and is summarized for each participant in Table 4.1. All names used in the study are pseudonyms.

Data were collected from six semi-structured interviews in Japanese, each of which lasted 45 to 90 minutes. Some specific questions asked in the interview were as follows: What kind of learning experience helps you try harder for EMI? Is there any learning experience that made you happy? Is there anything that you feel you have gained through taking EMI? What kind of learning experience decreases your motivation in EMI? Are there any EMI courses that you have dropped out of and, if so, why?

*Table 4.1* Demographic information from the survey data of Study 1

| Motivational Group | High | | Average | | Low | |
|---|---|---|---|---|---|---|
| Name | Michiko | Asa | Kaori | Yasuhiko | Ryoko | Hana |
| Grade | Senior | Junior | Senior | Junior | Junior | Freshman |
| Gender | Female | Female | Female | Male | Female | Female |
| TOEFL ITP | 520 | 487 | 500 | 450 | Over 550 | 460 |
| Experience of studying abroad | No | Yes | Yes | No | Returnee Yes | Yes |
| Understanding of the lectures (%) | 80 | 60 | 30 | 20 | 70 | 50 |
| Self-study time (hours) | 3 | 20 | 20 | 0 | 1 | 2 |
| Intended effort to learn English | 5.33 | 4.00 | 4.33 | 3.17 | 4.17 | 4.17 |
| Intended effort to learn content | 5.33 | 4.00 | 2.67 | 3.83 | 2.33 | 2.50 |
| EMI intrinsic motivation | 6.00 | 3.50 | 6.00 | 3.00 | 4.50 | 4.00 |

To analyze the interview data, a method of analysis based partly on Corbin and Strauss (2008), Strauss and Corbins' (1998) approach was employed.

(1) Spoken data were transcribed and reread. Data were then coded sentence by sentence or based on units of meaning.
(2) Creating concepts: The transcripts were read through once more, and concepts were created to describe each code. During this process, I made notes regarding interesting narratives and those relevant to SDT, the framework of the study. Concepts that were not directly related to the aim of this study, such as the participants' favorite stationery or their personal opinions about the relationship between Japan and the United States, were omitted.
(3) Creating categories: Concepts with a similar meaning were grouped and developed into categories. Then, categories from all participants' data were compared and combined.

Steps 2 and 3 were repeated throughout the process of analysis. The findings are described in the next section. In this chapter, categories are enclosed in angle brackets << >>, concepts in square brackets [ ], and in vivo codes, which are the participants' actual statements, in double quotes " ". Interviews were conducted in Japanese, but where actual statements from participants are used below, they have been translated by the author.

### Results and discussion: The harsh environment of EMI classes

The results of the data analysis yielded 150 concepts, which were developed into 10 categories (Table 4.2). The results suggest that the learning environment of EMI is harsh enough to hinder students' motivation.

The data reveal that the three psychological needs within the framework of SDT are not satisfied, especially the need for competence. Out of the 150 concepts, 86 are under Categories 1 <<English as a barrier to learning>> and 2 <<lack of self-efficacy>>, indicating that students are constantly getting implicit negative feedback on their performance, which leads to dissatisfaction of the need for competence (Vallerand & Reid, 1984). In addition, some other categories such as <<the need for relatedness unfulfilled>> and <<the need for autonomy unfulfilled>> show that none of the essential psychological needs are fulfilled. Finally, the third category, <<English as a barrier to belonging>>, reveal that the three psychological needs are interrelated as Ryan and Deci (2002) claimed and previous empirical studies revealed (Hiromori, 2005;

*Table 4.2* List of categories and concepts

---

**Category #1: English as a barrier to learning (80)**

*English as a barrier to voicing opinions (4)*

*Gaining less knowledge from EMI courses than courses conducted in Japanese (1)*

*Understanding part of a lecture that was not included in course materials or textbooks as a challenge (2)*

*International students' speech being too fast to comprehend (4)*

*Not experiencing a sense of improvement in English language abilities, even after getting good grades in EMI (1)*

*Writing in English as a challenge (6)*

*Lectures being too demanding to comprehend (7)*

*Reading in English as a challenge (6)*

*Understanding instructions in English as a challenge (2)*

*Regretting taking a challenging EMI course (3)*

*EMI taught by certain disciplinary instructors as a challenge, even after studying abroad (2)*

*EMI as a tough learning experience due to being unable to understand, despite trying hard (1)*

*Acquiring new knowledge in English as a challenge (3)*

*Learning academic vocabulary as a challenge (6)*

*Dropping out of EMI because of inability to understand EMI disciplinary instructors' lectures (2)*

*Writing essays in English as a challenge due to the inability to understand the teacher's expectations (1)*

*Taking notes in English as a challenge (5)*

*More focus required in EMI than lectures in Japanese (1)*

*Critical attitude towards EMI disciplinary instructors who do not speak clearly (2)*

*Difficulty retaining content learned in EMI (2)*

*Does not know which parts of the lectures are important unless they are emphasized by the EMI disciplinary instructors (1)*

*Loss of interest in media studies while postponing taking an EMI course due to lack of self-efficacy (1)*

*Giving up an EMI course that one really wanted to take due to lack of confidence in English writing ability (1)*

*Refusing to take a challenging EMI course for fear of being evaluated in the same way as native English speakers (1)*

*Withdrawing from a class if there is a high possibility of not being able to earn credits (1)*

---

*(continued)*

*Table 4.2* Cont.

| |
|---|
| *Nothing to gain from EMI due to lack of comprehension of the lectures (3)* |
| *Necessity of high English proficiency in order to enjoy EMI (1)* |
| *Group work with international students being exhausting due to difficulty communicating with them in English (10)* |

**Category #2: Lack of self-efficacy (6)**

| |
|---|
| *Not having efficient habits for studying (5)* |
| *Low evaluation of Japanese students, including oneself (1)* |

**Category #3: English as a barrier to belonging (7)**

| |
|---|
| *Feeling left out when everyone else is laughing at a teacher's joke (1)* |
| *High anxiety regarding learning with international students due to feeling inferior (1)* |
| *A sense of being inferior to TAs (1)* |
| *Feeling inferior to international students (4)* |

**Category #4: The need for relatedness unfulfilled (11)**

| |
|---|
| *Fear of asking questions due to an EMI disciplinary instructor seeming unapproachable (2)* |
| *Teaching assistant (TA) not being sympathetic (1)* |
| *Need to be brave enough to express opinions in English because of feeling that one's English is being judged by other Japanese students (4)* |
| *Collaborating with senpai as a challenge (1)* |
| *Group work with senpai as the most stressful task in an EMI preparatory course (1)* |
| *Difficulty in expressing opinions in group work with senpai (1)* |
| *Critical attitude towards EMI disciplinary instructors who do not know how to communicate with their students (1)* |

**Category #5: The need for autonomy unfulfilled (23)**

| |
|---|
| *Finding it unfair to be graded in the same way as international students (10)* |
| *Dissatisfaction with lectures that lack substantial content (not seeing the value of the course) (1)* |
| *Trying to get an A+ is not cost-effective considering the effort required (1)* |
| *Critical attitude towards EMI courses, which only assess students through exams (3)* |
| *Knowledge from EMI courses not being beneficial in the real world (3)* |
| *Not seeing the reason for learning about a poet while studying international relations (1)* |
| *Dropping out of a course that did not seem relevant (1)* |
| *Critical attitude towards EMI disciplinary instructors whose lectures were boring (1)* |
| *Critical attitude towards course content that does not follow the syllabus (1)* |

*Table 4.2* Cont.

Noticing there is a limit to copying others and the need to find one's own way of studying in EMI *(1)*

### Category #6: Heavy workload in EMI courses *(12)*

Need to find a balance with other classes taught in Japanese when taking EMI *(2)*

High amount of physical and psychological energy required to take EMI *(1)*

Being able to take a maximum of one or two challenging EMI courses for a maximum of one semester *(1)*

Selecting only EMI courses that one really wants to take due to a heavy workload *(1)*

Hesitating to take EMI due to a heavy workload *(2)*

Heavier workload required in EMI than courses taught in Japanese *(2)*

EMI being demanding *(1)*

Giving up an EMI course that one really wanted to take due to the expected overwhelming workload *(1)*

Giving up an EMI course that one really wanted to take as it seemed too demanding *(1)*

### Category #7: EMI as a burden *(3)*

EMI being extremely demanding for Japanese students *(2)*

EMI as a burden for many Japanese students *(1)*

### Category #8: Awareness of lack of interactions in EMI at University A *(1)*

Realizing that EMI at University A was not as interactive as classes in the USA *(1)*

### Category #9: The importance of autonomy-supportive teaching approaches in EMI *(5)*

EMI courses at University A will be more valuable for the students if they are designed to be more interactive *(1)*

Teacher's attitude determines how much students express their opinions *(1)*

Teachers can create an environment which is easy for Japanese students to express their opinions *(1)*

A non-judgmental attitude towards how students speak in English lets them voice their opinions with ease *(1)*

The important role of teachers' autonomy-supportive approach in stimulating students' intellectual interests *(1)*

### Category #10: A large class size as a barrier to learning *(2)*

Voicing their opinions as a challenge in a big lecture hall *(2)*

Note: The numbers in parentheses are the number of times that the concepts were mentioned. Such numbers are not usually counted in qualitative data analyses; however, to identify challenges that the participants were facing, I recorded the numbers as references.

Hiromori & Tanaka, 2006). The following sections describe each category, using students' statements to provide detail.

**Category 1: English as a barrier to learning.** Categories 1 and 2 make it clear that the need for competence is severely unfulfilled because it was repeatedly mentioned by everyone except Ryoko, a returnee from the United States. In fact, 86 concepts out of the 150 are related to dissatisfaction of the need for competence, such as Category 1, <<English as a barrier to learning>>, or Category 2, <<lack of self-efficacy>>.

Category 1, <<English as a barrier to learning>>, reveals how demanding EMI courses are for Japanese students. Most of the participants expressed that the need for competence is unfulfilled through several concepts, such as [English as a barrier to voicing opinions], [understanding instructions in English as a challenge], and [lectures being too demanding to comprehend]. Even Michiko, who was highly motivated, was [not experiencing a sense of improvement in English abilities, even after getting good grades in EMI].

*Excerpt 1*

Michiko     This (listening skill) is my weak point. Well … thanks to the teachers, they always give me good grades, but I do not feel I am doing that well.

Other concepts from Michiko and Hana suggested that the dissatisfaction of the need for competence was serious enough to cause amotivation. The following statements show that they were eager to take some EMI courses, but they could not do so because of the fear of being perceived as incompetent.

*Excerpt 2*

Michiko     Well, honestly, I want to take high-level EMI classes, but I have zero confidence about my ability to write in English including writing essays and short writing activities, so I balked.

*Excerpt 3*

Hana        I wanted to study media, and was going to take it, but the *senpai* (older students) stopped me. They insisted that I should not take it. They went like, "You shouldn't take media studies because it is too demanding!" So I followed their advice. I did not take media studies, and took developmental studies instead.

Researcher  Why don't you take media studies in the future?

Hana        Yes … maybe … well … I don't mind taking cultural sociology or something like that.

The following statements are some other examples of students not feeling competent in class. Asa took EMI courses to get ready to study abroad, and she always tried to volunteer to voice her opinions in class. Even a student like her, who had high motivation and relatively high English proficiency compared to the average TOEFL score among the participants, still struggled with actively participating in class.

*Excerpt 4*

Asa        I was sad when I bravely volunteered myself to voice my opinion, but could not convey my ideas. I felt so frustrated!!!
           I had lots of knowledge to share, but English, well, becomes a barrier, English did not let me express my ideas verbally.

The following comments by Yasuhiko and Kaori show how little they understood what was going on in class. They did not understand not only the content of the course but also the instructions in class.

*Excerpt 5*

Yasuhiko   I do not even understand what the questions meant in the exam, but I wrote a lot anyway.
           Well … so … the teacher may understand me trying to pass the course (from writing a lot).

*Excerpt 6*

Kaori      Well, the instructions and question in the exam … in fact, I am not sure if my understanding (of them) is a 100 percent correct.

***Category 2: Lack of self-efficacy.*** In this category, students express their low evaluation of their ability to learn. In Category 1, <<English as a barrier to learning>>, students' statements and stories are all about EMI lectures being demanding. On the other hand, in Category 2 <<lack of self-efficacy>>, they blame personal qualities for their failures in EMI. The following statement shows that their negative learning experiences in EMI are strong enough to worsen their low self-efficacy, which causes dissatisfaction of the need for competence.

*Excerpt 7*

Hana       Even if I follow the way of other good students to complete a task, I do not think I can perform well.
           It is because I have been slow, a slow learner, since I was a child. I called TAs numerous times, to teach me, but I still failed to complete the task.

*Category 3: English as a barrier to belonging.* Student dissatisfaction regarding the need for relatedness is expressed under the categories of <<the need for relatedness unfulfilled>>, and <<English as a barrier to belonging>>. The data show that Japanese students do not feel comfortable or supported in EMI. They feel lonely, nervous, and judged, not only by the EMI disciplinary instructors or TAs (teaching assistants), but also by their international and Japanese peers. Due to the unfulfillment of the need for relatedness, they do not ask questions or express themselves, even though it is important to satisfy the need for competence. Categories 3 and 4 also confirm that the three psychological needs are interrelated, and therefore, all of them are essential (Ryan & Deci, 2000). The following categories show how a sense of feeling incompetent makes one disconnect with the other class members and limits one's engagement. When everyone else was having fun, Yasuhiko had no idea why it was funny, so he felt isolated and ignored.

*Excerpt 8*

Yasuhiko     I rarely understand what the teacher is saying. Well, in a typical situation like the teacher makes a joke and everyone laughs. I do not follow that at all.

Also, Kaori, Hana, and Michiko were isolated because of their [feeling inferior to international students], which is categorized under <<English as a barrier to belonging>>. The following excerpts illustrate this.

*Excerpt 9*

Hana     Well, in class, international students were following the class with no problem and understanding what was going on quickly.
But I did not understand (the class) and, well, did not know what I should do, and felt overwhelmed.

*Excerpt 10*

Kaori     I entered this university as a Japanese student. I wanted to be equal to the international students.
Well, now, at University A, it is true that Japanese students fall behind, and international students succeed.

*Excerpt 11*

Researcher     Is there anything you feel that is difficult or challenging when taking EMI?

| Michiko | Group work with the international students is … exhausting … In reality, no matter what I do, I cannot follow people who speak native-like English. Well … it creates an uncomfortable atmosphere.<br>They go like "Don't you understand this?" … Yeah, well, actually I cannot work with people who have that kind of attitude. |
|---|---|

*Excerpt 12*

| Researcher | Do you have any anxiety to take EMI? |
|---|---|
| Hana | Yes. Well … The international students are proactive, such as in voicing their opinions.<br>They strongly express their opinions in group work, don't they? I might go silent in a group. (I am worried) I may not be able to belong there.<br>(The international students will say) like, "Again, Japanese students can't speak" … "Yeah, Japanese can't speak." |

Excerpts 11 and 12 demonstrate that Japanese students have high anxiety about working with international students. Japanese students feel that the international students do not want to work with them because Japanese students are not fluent enough in English. The feeling of being inferior to the international students is actually consistent with EMI disciplinary instructors evaluating the international students higher than Japanese students, as mentioned at the beginning of this book. This suggests that the University A EMI classrooms have a culture that creates a hierarchy, where those who are more fluent in English are in power. That is why they not only feel like they do not belong, but also feel actively disrespected by international students. This section shows that Japanese students feel they are not good enough, and not welcome in EMI classrooms.

***Category 4: The need for relatedness unfulfilled.*** Concepts placed in the category <<the need for relatedness unfulfilled>> express the interrelationship between the need for relatedness and competence. To illustrate, Kaori did not ask questions, even though she wanted to, because she thought the EMI disciplinary instructor was a "frightening person". This also indicates that she did not feel safe or connected with the EMI disciplinary instructor, so she could not ask questions to foster understanding about the coursework, which could have otherwise led to the fulfillment of the need for competence.

*Excerpt 13*

| Kaori | Well, Mr. Yoshimoto (teacher pseudonym) is, well … no. Can't ask questions of him, can I? Especially Mr. Yoshimoto … who is that frightening. He is scary. |
|---|---|

Hana also expressed a strong sense of dissatisfaction regarding the need for relatedness with her peers and TAs in an EMI preparatory course only for the Japanese students. Her dissatisfaction of the need for relatedness suppressed her self-efficacy, categorized as <<the need for relatedness unfulfilled>>. Interestingly, this suggests a complex power balance among Japanese students in EMI. Hana said that she needed [to be brave enough to express opinions because of feeling that one's English is being judged] by other Japanese students. Her anxiety about being criticized was strong enough to stop her from answering questions voluntarily in EMI.

*Excerpt 14*

Hana       Well, I actually hesitate to speak in English. In fact, speaking in English in front of Japanese requires tremendous courage because I care that they may think like, "Is what you are saying grammatically correct?"
They (other Japanese students) may be judging my English, well, they think I am not good at speaking or things like that.
I actually care a lot about how they think about me.

This issue is exacerbated by the strong age hierarchy common in Japanese social situations. In schools for example, *kohai* (younger students) are under intense social pressure to defer to their *senpai* (older students), who often take on a kind of mentorship or leadership role by default, simply by virtue of their age. In addition, she mentioned [group work with *senpai* as the most stressful task in an EMI preparatory course], because they tried to "fix" her opinions whenever she voiced them. Therefore, she gradually found it difficult to express her opinions in front of them.

*Excerpt 15*

Hana       Well, the group presentation was the hardest in the EMI preparatory class.

Researcher    Would you describe it more?

Hana       Well, yeah, I was the only freshman in my group, so I should not stand out too much.

And actually, many of the *senpai* (in the group) were quite experienced. Well, s/he actually knew (many things).
Although I had things which I wanted to share, and put my opinions out there, the *senpai* went like "Well, there are more things that you don't see in this" and "fixed" my opinions.
Well, I appreciated it, but in fact, expressing my opinions became hard.

Hana had another issue while working with older students. One *senpai* who was sophomore had lower English competence than her and so she wanted to help them present in English. However, she could not correct their grammar mistakes due to the age difference.

*Excerpt 16*

Hana   It was challenging to do a group presentation.
     [...] Well, I am a freshman, and they are sophomores. Their transcriptions for the presentation were a huge mess.
     They did not know what they wanted to say, and there were some sentences (on the scripts) which did not seem like complete sentences. But I was not able to point out the mistakes because they were my *senpai(s)*.

As described in this category, not having a trustworthy relationship with others in EMI courses took away from Hana opportunities to experience a sense of achievement and growth. Furthermore, she complained about a TA who was neither sympathetic nor helpful.

*Excerpt 17*

Hana   People who can excel in everything [like the TA] may not be able to understand why other people cannot.
     The TA said that it was easy, but it might not be easy for me. They suggested study techniques, but I realized that, at the end of the day, I needed to discover my own study techniques.

**Category 5: The need for autonomy unfulfilled.** Finally, the need for autonomy is also found to be unfulfilled. The most frequent complaints that related to the need for autonomy are about how students are assessed. Michiko repeatedly mentioned [finding it unfair to be graded in the same way as international students]. She said this happened because international students were already fluent in English, whereas Japanese students were still in the process of learning English. Thus, she believed that these two groups needed to be graded differently.

*Excerpt 18*

Michiko  Once we take EMI, it is like everyone is really in the same arena till the end of the course.

     It is demanding for Japanese students. Well ... many of the courses are half-baked which is not interesting enough for international students (but tough for the Japanese students).

     [...] In the future, one class could have various grading systems to adapt the courses for diverse levels of the students.

| Researcher | Do you mean regarding English proficiency? |
|---|---|
| Michiko | Yes, regarding English proficiency<br>A little bit … well … fill the gap and make taking EMI easier for everyone … something like giving us more options. |

Since the objectives of EMI do not include teaching English, the consequent evaluation should not be based on its fluency. However, at least from the students' perspectives, proficiency in English influences their grades. The inadequate teaching skills of EMI disciplinary instructors might be a contributing factor to this scenario (Macaro et al., 2019). Many of them have little or no training to teach language learners, which affects their evaluation of students' performance (Hernández-Nanclares & Jimènez-Muñoz, 2017). This indicates the inability of EMI instructors to separate students' English proficiency and their ideas. Consequently, the Japanese students cannot attain better grades than the international students. Michiko's story reveals that the Japanese students might have already realized this, and that is why they felt it was unfair.

Ryoko and Yasuhiro expressed a [critical attitude towards EMI courses, which only assess students through exams]. They felt that the EMI disciplinary instructors did not value their effort or participation.

*Excerpt 19*

| Ryoko | I take a look at syllabi because I want to know what the class will be really about especially the grading system … well … how the teacher gives us grades. |
|---|---|
| Researcher | Do you have any particular point of the grading system you take a look at when you choose a class? |
| Ryoko | Well, my very least favorite does exist at University A.<br>There are courses in which 50 percent of the grade is based on the midterm exam and the other 50 percent is based on the final exam.<br><br>In this kind of course, if I perform badly in either one of the exams, I will be really failing, well, there is a possibility that I will be really failing.<br><br>I would like the teachers to see the attendance and the ability to join discussions. |

*Excerpt 20*

| Yasuhiko | I don't care if the teachers care if we attend … but well …<br>That 50 percent of the grade is based on the midterm and the other 50 percent is based on the final exam is a little bit …<br>Like having quizzes … I wish there was a way out not to fail. |
|---|---|

The next two categories, Category 6 <<heavy workload in EMI courses>> and Category 7 <<EMI as a burden>> represent EMI disciplinary instructors' unrealistic expectations of the Japanese students. Students tend to take minimal credits in EMI because, unfortunately, they develop negative attitudes toward EMI when taking EMI courses. Many of the EMI disciplinary instructors tend to compare the workload that they give in their EMI courses to the workload that they took on as students in their master's or even PhD courses in English-speaking countries. Again, maybe that is the only way for them to design their courses without appropriate teacher training. Nevertheless, it is also true that it is neither professional nor realistic to think that Japanese undergraduate students can tackle those courses. In addition, students feel that EMI disciplinary instructors do not provide adequate explanations of why they are teaching what they teach, so they do not see the value in striving to grasp course content. The following excerpt shows that students consider [knowledge from EMI courses as not being beneficial in the real world].

*Excerpt 21*

**Kaori**     **I cannot make enough time to study for EMI because I have to know various other things … knowledge which is necessary for living in the society**.

As a consequence, EMI has become an obligation for the Japanese students to graduate. The following two categories show that they are exhausted by the requirement to obtain 20 credits through EMI courses.

***Category 6: Heavy workload in EMI courses.*** The following excerpt from Kaori shows that she was struggling with EMI even after a year of studying abroad. Since not everyone at University A studies abroad, it is easy to imagine many Japanese students having similar or even harder experiences in EMI.

*Excerpt 22*

**Kaori**     **Well, taking EMI is an extremely high hurdle to jump for the Japanese students. Even after studying abroad, Yoshimoto-sensei's and Chang-sensei's classes were challenging.
Well, one class, I could take one or two challenging courses. That is fine with me. But if I take more than that, it will be over my head.**

Another excerpt from Kaori reveals that since EMI is too demanding for Japanese students, it discourages many from taking more EMI than they absolutely have to. EMI instructors care about their courses not being too easy for the international students, but on flip side, their courses are losing Japanese students.

*Excerpt 23*

Kaori          **Well, think about taking a balance and take only EMI courses,
               which I truly want to take. Yeah, (taking EMI is) demanding,
               demanding.**

*Category 7: EMI as a burden.* This category illustrates that [EMI is a
burden to Japanese students].

*Excerpt 24*

Michiko        **Well … actually, many Japanese students have failed EMI
               courses, so I have never seen anyone who is willing to take EMI
               courses more than they needed except me.
               Obtaining 20 credits from EMI looks like such a high hurdle to
               jump. That is why, how to set a bar lower, and how to educate the
               students to overcome the challenges in EMI and transform them
               to eagerly take it, is something that the university should think
               about. Having to get 20 credits from EMI seems a burden to
               every Japanese student.**

From EMI instructors' perspectives, Japanese students are the ones
not meeting their expectations. However, Japanese students suggest that
University A reconsider the EMI curricular because it is not working. In
fact, Asa, who was studying abroad when her interview was conducted,
realized that the EMI disciplinary instructors needed to apply better
pedagogical approaches if they wanted their students to be more
engaged and motivated. She suggested that EMI instructors were not
meeting students' expectations either, because of a lack of interactions
and supportive teaching approaches in EMI.

*Category 8: Awareness of lack of interactions in EMI at University
A.* Asa was studying in the United States at the time of the interview
and reported [realizing that EMI at University A is not as interactive as
classes in the United States].

*Excerpt 25*

Asa            **Well, University A's classes are interactive compare to other
               courses taught in Japan, but I realized that actually it was not at
               all through taking classes here (the US).
               Classes (at University A, and the university in the US) were both
               conducted in English, but compared to the US, EMI courses at
               University A are not there yet, not interactive enough because
               students have only few opportunities to participate.
               EMI courses at University A will be more valuable if EMI there
               could become even a little more interactive … well, even a little
               bit more.**

*Category 9: The Importance of autonomy-supportive teaching approaches in EMI.* Asa also came to believe in the <<importance of autonomy-supportive teaching approaches in EMI >> to make EMI more interactive at University A. This can be illustrated by her experience in the United States.

*Excerpt 26*

Asa        For example, I am the only exchange student in my class now, well, there is one more Chinese student, but everyone else is American. The teachers said, "I want to hear valuable opinions from the minorities. I make mistakes, I welcome mistakes. Actually, not voicing opinions is a mistake."
           Thanks to that, well … He said he was not a native speaker, and I was not either, but listeners were native speakers, so they should be able to guess what we meant. It has been very easy for me to volunteer to share my opinions because of what he said.

*Excerpt 27*

Asa        Well, I don't want to study anymore; it is not fun, or not interesting when the atmosphere of the class becomes so that students can't say anything but the right answer.
           I guess, actually, how teachers design their class is a big deal for the students. Well, how they create their classrooms influences (our curiosity). I could grow my academic interests with things that I was not interested in before (if the teacher is good). Students have to try their best, but how hard they can try depends on the teachers.

The belief that it was totally acceptable not to be perfect encouraged Asa tremendously in terms of expressing her opinions in class. She had attended this teacher's class before the interview and enthusiastically mentioned that she had volunteered to answer a question that day as well. She insisted that students could be more proactive when they knew that their instructors would accept answers and value students' input, even if their opinions were not perfectly presented or different from the teachers' expectations. She found that the [teacher's attitude determines how much students voice their opinions].

Her stories confirm the importance of teachers accepting students' perspectives to fulfill the need for autonomy, thereby enhancing students' motivation. However, EMI classrooms at University A are not autonomy-supportive learning environments for Japanese students.

*Category 10: A large class size as a barrier to learning.* The last category reveals that having a couple of hundred students in one classroom is an obstacle for language learners to participate actively in class.

*Excerpt 28*

Asa         Well, first of all, speaking about volunteering to share my opinions, if I sit in the back of the classroom, I have to see 200 students. But if I sit at the front seat, I will see some of the students, well only some of the students who are sitting in front of me. I am also closer to the teacher when I am at the front seat ... sitting at a back seat makes it (voicing my opinion) even more challenging.

The following story shows that even Ryoko, who had high English proficiency, felt that expressing her opinion was demanding in a big lecture hall.

*Excerpt 29*

Ryoko       I was not able to volunteer to share my opinions that often in the US, too. I was only able to do so when I had extremely strong feelings to do so. Back in University A, it is worse ... because of having a class in a big lecture hall; I do not want to do that.

As we have seen in the EMI context, English is an obstacle to learning for Japanese students (dissatisfaction of the need for perceived competence). Moreover, they do not feel valued or heard as important individuals (dissatisfaction of the need for perceived autonomy), in addition to feeling alienated (dissatisfaction of the need for perceived relatedness). In such an unsatisfying learning environment, it is natural that students' motivation and learning are not fostered.

To rescue Japanese students from such a harsh environment, pedagogical interventions need to be implemented to help them comprehend lectures better and fulfill the three psychological needs, subsequently boosting their EMI intrinsic motivation and cultivating their extrinsic motivation into a more autonomous one.

## Designing pedagogical interventions: Inspiration from students' comments

The results of the qualitative study not only highlighted students' difficulties and motivation issues, they also hinted at ways in which the situation could be improved. To obtain concrete ideas to design possible pedagogical interventions, the interview data in Study 2 were reanalyzed to explore students' preferred teaching approaches. Doing so was necessary to further fulfill their need for autonomy. This section will outline when the students felt achievement/enjoyment and when they faced setbacks in EMI classrooms. Based on my previous experience designing pedagogical interventions for EMI courses (Kojima et al., 2013), these moments were seen to highlight the support students need.

As a result of these analyses, 14 student statements were categorized into six requests for designing pedagogical interventions, including various formats. The requests, which were extracted from the interviews and coded, are shown below with excerpts.

(1) Desire to communicate with international students.

*Excerpt 30*

| | |
|---|---|
| Kaori | Taking the EMI course [peace studies] was extremely interesting because the international students voiced some opinions that were different from my expectations. I think this [learning what is happening in the world today from real-life stories] happened only in EMI, which had a diverse student body. |

*Excerpt 31*

| | |
|---|---|
| Yasuhiko | I was happy when I received an opportunity to communicate in EMI courses. |
| Researcher | Communicate with the teacher? Or … ? |
| Yasuhiko | Communicate with the students. Several EMI courses have often involved some group work. During the group work, I had to communicate with the international students as I had expected. Actually, it was more than I had expected … speaking to someone for the first time in English is not something I have experienced very often. Therefore, becoming friends with them, conversing with them about various things, and learning from them was good for me. |

*Excerpt 32*

| | |
|---|---|
| Asa | EMI courses are extremely active [compared to the courses conducted in Japanese]. In addition, at University A, the students come from different countries, so I am able to listen to opinions from different perspectives. I find EMI tremendously fun. |

(2) Desire to receive academic writing instructions.

*Excerpt 33*

| | |
|---|---|
| Asa | When we submitted our outline a week before we had to submit our midterm essay assignment, the teacher provided us feedback about it. Thus, I knew how I would have to improve my writing while working on my essay. |

*Excerpt 34*

Michiko    Well ... I would love to take EMI courses with high academic standards. [Regarding] writing an essay in English, ... I am still not at all confident about writing an essay, so I have avoided taking these EMI courses.

*Excerpt 35*

Hana    Well ... writing an essay ... I had to choose a topic; then, I had to make some connections between the topic and my experiences and write about it. However, I did not know how to do it. In order to complete the assignment, I approached the teacher, *senpai*, and friends who spoke better English for advice.

(3)  Desire for interactive EMI.

*Excerpt 36*

Asa    In EMI, the teacher often asked the students for their opinions. Well, the EMI classes did not have a one-way lecture style. The teacher asked questions and the students answered them.

*Excerpt 37*

Asa    Well, after all, expressing my opinions in EMI made me happy, although volunteering my opinions took courage.

(4)  Desire to access PowerPoint slides for self-study.

*Excerpt 38*

Michiko    When I can access the PowerPoint slides in advance, I can study at home before class, but if they are not available, there is no other way to prepare for the lecture.

*Excerpt 39*

Asa    The instructor uploaded the PowerPoint slides the day before each class. Therefore, I scanned them and reread some parts of the textbook that I found difficult to understand.

(5)  Desire to obtain glossaries for reading.

*Excerpt 41*

Hana    For vocabulary that I did not know ... well, I thought I should try to look up all the new vocabulary words in a dictionary, so I did ... For me, reading the textbook was a demanding experience.

*Excerpt 42*

Yasuhiko    When I take an EMI course, I find it overwhelming to learn too
            many new words.

*Excerpt 43*

Michiko     I knew I would have to go through the reading assignments
            thoroughly [in order to take the final exam], but I couldn't ...
            Reading the textbook was too demanding for me to complete
            because of my poor English proficiency.

6. Desire to ask questions in Japanese.

*Excerpt 44*

Yasuhiko    To some degree, I thought I could ask questions in Japanese
            because the instructor was Japanese. That is why I took this
            course.

The above requests were referred to when designing the series of
pedagogical interventions. The rest of this chapter briefly discusses how
each suggestion was adopted for the pedagogical interventions which
will be explained in detail in Chapter 5.

First, as many excerpts illustrate, the students wanted to communicate with the international students in EMI. Hence, I decided to ensure
that every Japanese student would have such opportunities by creating
small, fixed groups with international students. In addition, writing
an essay seemed to be a challenging task, so a preparatory tutorial
session for the final exam was offered as a writing support. Students
also pointed out that good EMI courses were interactive. Thus, online
discussion forums were used to increase student–teacher interactions.
The data also revealed that students used PowerPoint slides that the
EMI disciplinary instructors had created for their lectures for self-study.
However, the EMI disciplinary instructor that I worked with during the
pedagogical interventions preferred not to use them in class. Therefore,
some comprehension check questions were posted weekly on the online
learning system to foster student comprehension to compensate for
PowerPoint slides not being distributed.

Regarding the distribution of a glossary and letting students communicate with each other in Japanese, such requests were only adopted
in Cultural Studies. This is because, based on my experience conducting
previous pedagogical interventions (Kojima et al., 2013), a glossary
created by someone who is not the course instructor has limited effectiveness. On the other hand, the reading assignment for Cultural Studies
had a large number of technical terms, so I expected that students

would struggle to understand it. Thus, glossaries were made for that course to help them tackle the reading. The use of Japanese was discouraged because the EMI disciplinary instructor was concerned about international students' possible complaints about the peda-gogical interventions to support only Japanese students. Nevertheless, in Gender Studies only a few students were able to post their opinions in online discussion forums in English. This meant that extra scaffolding was required to help Japanese students be more active. Thus, after discussing it with the EMI disciplinary lecturer, extra online discussion forums were created in Japanese to support their learning in Cultural Studies.

## The necessity of pedagogical interventions

This chapter explores how Japanese students feel in actual EMI classrooms. Their stories show that they feel inadequate when taking EMI and left behind (unfulfillment of the need for competence), not respected as important individuals (unfulfillment of the need for autonomy), and disconnected from the community (need for related-ness). This means that none of the three psychological needs within SDT are satisfied, and thereby students are unable to commit to studying for EMI courses. These results shed light on the necessity for pedagogical interventions to alter this harsh social environment for Japanese students. In the interviews, participants also expressed their expectations and preferred teaching approaches, such as their desire to communicate with international students, to receive academic writing instruction, and to make EMI more interactive. Such ideas were referenced when designing the series of pedagogical interventions, to save Japanese students from this severe learning environment and enhance their learning in EMI.

## References

Corbin, J., & Strauss, A. (2008). *Basics of qualitative research: Techniques and procedures for developing grounded theory* (3rd ed.). Sage. https://doi.org/10.4135/9781452230153

Hernandez-Nanclares, N., & Jimenez-Munoz, A. (2017). English as a medium of instruction: Evidence for language and content targets in bilingual education in economics. *International Journal of Bilingual Education and Bilingualism*, *20*(7), 883–896. https://doi.org/10.1080/13670050.2015.1125847

Hiromori, T. (2005). Three factors that motivate L2 learners: From the perspectives of general tendency and individual differences. *JACET Bulletin*, *41*, 37–50.

Hiromori, T., & Tanaka, H. (2006). Instructional intervention on motivating English learners: The self-determination theory viewpoint. *Language Education and Technology, 43*, 111–126.

Kojima, N., Sato, Y., & Hamciuc, M. (2013). Nihonjingakusei no eigo baitai niyoru gakkagakushu to team teaching—Ritsumeikan Asia Pacific University ni okeru bridge course no kokoromi [Japanese students' learning experiences in English-medium and team teaching—A project in a bridge course at Ritsumeikan Asia Pacific University]. *Polyglossia, 24*, 210–223.

Macaro, D., Jimenez-Munoz, A., & Lasagabaster, D. (2019). The importance of certification of English Medium Instruction teachers in higher education in Spain. *Porta Linguarum, 32*, 103–118.

Ryan, R. M., & Deci, E. L. (2000). Self-determination theory and the facilitation of intrinsic motivation, social development, and well-being. *American Psychologist, 55*(1), 68–78. https://doi.org/10.1037/0003-066x.55.1.68

Ryan, R. M., & Deci, E. L. (2002). An overview of self-determination theory: An organismic-dialectical perspective. In E. L. Deci & R. M. Ryan (Eds.), *Handbook of self-determination research* (pp. 3–33). University of Rochester Press.

Strauss, A., & Corbin, J. (1998). *Basics of qualitative research: Techniques and procedures for developing grounded theory* (2nd ed.). Sage.

Vallerand, R. J., & Reid, G. (1984). On the causal effects of perceived competence on intrinsic motivation: A test of cognitive evaluation theory. *Journal of Sport Psychology, 6*, 94–102.

# 5 Pedagogical interventions to motivate students

A series of pedagogical interventions were conducted in two English-medium instruction (EMI) courses at University A (Gender Studies and Cultural Studies) to enhance students' comprehension of the lectures and to enhance their motivation by fulfilling the three psychological needs (i.e., the needs for autonomy, competence, and relatedness) of self-determination theory (SDT). The pedagogical interventions were of various types and were employed at different times throughout the course. They included assigning students to small groups with international students, utilizing online discussion forums and providing a preparatory session for the final exam. One Japanese professor in area studies taught both courses in which the interventions were employed. She was willing to collaborate with me because she knew the importance of faculty development in pedagogy, particularly in classrooms with diverse needs. She was also aware of Japanese students' lower pass rates and performances compared to the international students in EMI. Each course comprised 14 classes and a final exam over a period of seven weeks (see Table 5.1 for an overview of the series of pedagogical interventions). A quantitative study in Gender Studies and a qualitative study in both Gender Studies and Cultural Studies were conducted to examine the impact of the pedagogical interventions. This chapter describes the pedagogical interventions first and reports the quantitative study to examine the impacts of the interventions.

My role in Gender Studies and Cultural Studies was a combination of English teacher/ researcher. I observed more than half the course and helped students when they had a hard time following the lectures. On the other hand, I told the students I was not going to be involved in grading. I planned and conducted the series of pedagogical interventions, but the lesson plans were completely made by the EMI disciplinary instructor.

In the beginning, the EMI disciplinary instructor was concerned about the international students' reactions. She predicted that some of them might feel it was unfair if they thought that only the Japanese students would be getting extra help. To proactively address this issue, the pedagogical interventions involved everyone in the class, including international students. In addition, the objectives of the series of the pedagogical interventions and the details were explained in the syllabi, as well as orally at the beginning of each course. Consequently, the international students made no complaints related to the pedagogical interventions.

## The pedagogical interventions from the perspective of SDT

### *The need for autonomy*

Fulfilling the need for autonomy is critical in educational contexts (Reeve, 2002). It can be achieved by understanding the classroom from the students' perspective. This means that any interventions that involve listening to students' accounts and acting upon their opinions are already autonomously supportive to some degree. With the theoretical background discussed in Chapter 2 in mind, the following measures were implemented in both the Gender Studies and Cultural Studies courses to help fulfill the need for autonomy.

(1) *An orientation for the interventions.* The orientation lasted about 10 minutes and was presented in a lecture-style format. It explained the aims of the series of pedagogical interventions and how they would help deepen learning for all the students, not just Japanese students. Sharing how the pedagogical interventions were valuable for learning helped everyone see its significance.

(2) *A student course-evaluation session.* After the midterm exam during lesson seven, the EMI disciplinary instructor left the classroom. Then, the students, the TAs, and I discussed what the students liked about the course and things they wanted the EMI disciplinary instructor to change. Afterward, the TAs and I shared some of the most frequent suggestions with the disciplinary instructor. The purpose of this session was to create a space where students could express their doubts or negative feelings about the course without external pressure.

(3) *An online discussion forum in English.* Students were welcome to ask any questions, give recommendations for the course and share what they knew about the course content at any time. To encourage them to post their comments and to promote their interest in the content, I expressed my appreciation to the students by replying to

most of the comments individually. Furthermore, I shared some supplemental websites. Again, the goal was to create a community for the students where they could be honest with their opinions and emotions, even negative ones. In addition, my contact information was on the syllabus so that they could contact me (in either Japanese or English) at any time. I set it up this way because I thought that some students might prefer to share their thoughts privately.

(4) ***Online discussion forums in Japanese.*** In Cultural Studies, online discussion forums in Japanese were created. In Gender Studies, online discussion forums in Japanese were not utilized, and there were only a few students who posted their comments there. It indicated that a little more scaffolding should be provided. Thus, aiming to help them practice posting their comments without a language barrier, online discussions forums in Japanese were offered in Cultural Studies. In the online discussion forums, students were asked to share their anxieties and worries as well as things they could not follow during the lectures. I stated that comments not directly related to the content were also welcome (e.g., communication problems with classmates, concerns about one's English). This was intended to boost the need for autonomy as well as to satisfy the need for relatedness, which will be discussed later in this chapter.

### The need for competence

The qualitative study to explore how students were feeling in EMI discussed in Chapter 4 (Study 2) uncovered that Japanese students' need for competence appeared to be severely unsatisfied. To boost the students' understanding and let them experience a sense of growth and accomplishment, the following learning supports were provided.

(1) ***A session for developing reading skills in English.*** To help students tackle the reading assignments for the course, skills for effective reading in English were presented for approximately five minutes during the first lesson. This included encouraging students to read the title, topic, and concluding sentences first, then check terminological definition and obtain background knowledge in their first language (L1), as well as in English. The students were also encouraged to share with their peers what they did and did not understand, because doing so would advance their comprehension of the reading texts.

(2) *A preparatory tutorial session for the final exam.* Students expressed that explicit instructions and constructive feedback from the teachers were necessary to tackle EMI writing assignments in Study 2 (Chapter 4). To help them write and thus fulfill their need for competence, an optional preparatory tutorial session for the final exam was offered. It lasted for about one class period (95 minutes) and was held a day before the final exam (between lessons 14 and 15); the teaching assistants (TAs) and I provided writing instructions to the students individually.

During the preparatory tutorial session for the final exam, oral instructions were primarily given in Japanese, while the handouts I created were written in English. To reinforce the session's effectiveness, I had an hour-long meeting with the EMI disciplinary instructor and the TAs before the tutorial session. This allowed me to understand exactly what the EMI disciplinary instructor was looking for in terms of writing and how best to improve students' exam scores, thus ensuring better overall grades for the course as the final exam comprised 50 percent of their grade.

(3) *Small groups with international students.* Everyone was assigned to fixed groups of three or four students throughout the course. I expected that being in small groups would encourage the students to ask each other questions (to promote their comprehension of the lectures) and fulfill their need for relatedness, which will be discussed later in this chapter.

(4) *Online discussion forums in English.* Either a comprehension check question or a task based on the week's lecture was posted weekly to increase the students' self-study time, thus fostering their learning. Additionally, the EMI disciplinary instructor preferred not to use PowerPoint slides or did not have time to create reading guides for the students. Therefore, I suggested posting comprehension check questions, and she agreed. I replied to each student with informational rewards (e.g., showing my appreciation for sharing their thoughts, praising their comments) and positive feedback. In addition to communicating with individuals, whenever I could not participate in a lesson, I gave some compliments on their performance or advice on their learning to everyone on the discussion forums.

(5) *Glossary.* The students claimed that the vocabulary of reading assignments in EMI was challenging. Also, a study conducted in the Gulf Arab region, Malcolm (2013) found that students in EMI courses, even when their English proficiency is high, still struggle with terminology. However, a glossary was not provided for Gender

Studies because I wanted to focus on learning support to make it applicable to future EMI courses. On the contrary, the content of the reading assignments in Cultural Studies might have been less familiar to students than that of Gender Studies, which contributed to its challenging nature. Therefore, I conducted vocabulary analyses and created glossaries for each unit of the reading assignments in Cultural Studies. I asked the EMI disciplinary instructor for advice to minimize the amount of vocabulary listed when the drafts were made. Subsequently, they were shared with everyone via the online learning system before classes began.

### The need for relatedness

As described in the previous chapter, the fulfillment of the need for relatedness is crucial in educational contexts (Ryan & Powelson, 1991). The following measures were taken to fulfill this need.

(1) **Small groups with international students.** As explained previously, all Japanese students were in a fixed group of three or four with international students throughout the course. This was done to create a community for everyone to belong to and rely on, so they could feel connected to others in the classroom, in addition to fulfilling their need for competence.
(2) **Online discussion forums in Japanese.** The online discussion forums in Japanese were implemented not only to meet the need for autonomy but also the need for relatedness. Asking students to voice their thoughts and emotions in Japanese was a way to show them empathy, and to acknowledge their emotions. The Japanese TAs and I shared our experiences as language learners and tried to make personal connections with the students, hoping to let them know we cared about them.

## Study 3: Changing motivational orientations with pedagogical interventions

### Research questions and context

To investigate motivational changes through the series of pedagogical interventions, a quantitative study, Study 3, was conducted. The study asked the following four research questions.

(1) Is it possible to enhance EMI intrinsic motivation, decrease amotivation, and internalize extrinsic motivation in Japanese students through educational interventions intended to fulfill the three psychological needs of SDT in the EMI context?

(2) Is it possible to enhance motivation to learn English (i.e., intended effort to learn English, attitude to learning English, ideal L2 self and ought-to L2 self) and intended effort to learn content through the pedagogical interventions?

(3) Is it possible to increase students' comprehension of the lectures and promote their self-study time through the pedagogical interventions?

(4) Are there students who developed different motivational trajectories during the course wherein the pedagogical interventions were implemented? If so, how did students experience the course differently?

Gender Studies was an elective course for sophomores or upper-level undergraduates in the social studies department. A disciplinary instructor, three teaching assistants, and I were involved in the pedagogical interventions. The EMI disciplinary instructor provided all the class lessons. While I was not involved in planning or giving lessons, I planned and conducted all the aspects of the pedagogical interventions. One of the TAs was Vietnamese and was hired by the university, while the other two, who were Japanese, were the EMI disciplinary instructor's seminar students and participated voluntarily. All of them were fluent in English and Japanese and were familiar with the Gender Studies' course content. The five of us held debriefings each week, which were conducted both in English and Japanese.

All the lessons were conducted in English, and class materials were written in English. In addition, the students communicated in English with the EMI disciplinary instructor, the TAs, and me, both in the classroom and outside scheduled class time.

*Method*

Data were collected from Gender Studies during the first quarter and Cultural Studies during the second quarter. However, only 21 Japanese students were left in Cultural Studies after the students who enrolled in both courses were eliminated. Of these 21 students, only 15 answered both pre- and post- surveys. Thus, the data for the quantitative research in this chapter only includes Gender Studies. Whereas, the data for qualitative study in Chapter 6 includes both Gender Studies and Cultural Studies.

Two hundred and thirty-four students registered for the course, and 60 of whom were Japanese. Out of the 60, six students never attended, so 54 Japanese students took the pre- survey, while only 38 out of the 54 took the post- survey (seven males and 31 females). This means that 30 percent of the students dropped out at some point during the course. In addition, 14 students attended the preparatory tutorial session for the final exam, described earlier; 11 of the 14 participants answered both the pre- and post- surveys. The responses of the 38 students were then analyzed. The mean score of the self-reported TOEFL ITP was 483 ($SD$ = 40.84); the highest score was 550, and the lowest was 410.

Two questionnaires were administered during the quarter (at Times 1 and 3, as shown in Table 5.1). In addition, students reported their average percentage of understanding of the EMI lectures (at Times 1, 2, and 3) as well as their average self-study time per week (at Times 2 and 3) throughout the quarter. The pre-questionnaire was administered during Lesson 1 (at Time 1), and the post-questionnaire during Lesson 14 (at Time 3). All the data were collected during class time. Given university restrictions, I could not conduct the post-questionnaire during the final exam. Therefore, the post-questionnaire was carried out during Lesson 14, the last lesson before the final exam. Doing so meant that the post-questionnaire was conducted before the preparatory tutorial session for the final exam; its influence (if any) was thus not reflected in the questionnaire results. To compensate, students who took part in the final exam preparatory session were asked to fill out an evaluation sheet for it at the end.

For the questionnaire design, several measures from prior research were used in this study. All the items explained below were rated using a 6-point Likert scale, adapted from Hiromori (2006) and Yashima et al. (2009), which are Japanese versions of the studies carried out by Noels et al. (2000), to understand Canadian university students' motivation to learn French. To fit the EMI contexts, minor changes were made, such as replacing the word "English" with "EMI." In addition, self-reported TOEFL ITP scores were requested on the pre-questionnaire, and the evaluation of the series of pedagogical intervention was included on the post-questionnaire. The pre-survey consisted of a total of 64 items, and the post-survey consisted of a total of 69 items. In the description below, the first Cronbach's α listed is for the pre-questionnaire, while the second is for the post-questionnaire.

Four items each to assess students' EMI intrinsic motivation (e.g., "EMI lectures are exciting") (Cronbach's α = .88, .80), EMI identified

*Table 5.1* Overview of class schedule, intervention, and data collection

| Lesson | 1 | 2–6 | 7 | 8–13 | 14 | 15 |
|---|---|---|---|---|---|---|
| Class lesson | Course orientation | Lecture | Midterm test | Lecture | Student presentations | Final exam |
| Pedagogical intervention | An orientation for the intervention A session for developing reading skills in English An orientation for the online discussion forum | | Student evaluation session (20 minutes) | | | Preparatory tutorial session for the final exam (95 minutes) |
| | Small group with international students Online discussion forum | | | | | |
| Data collection | (Time 1) Pre-questionnaire: | | (Time 2) Participants' self-reported understanding of the lecture and self-study time | | (Time 3) Post-questionnaire: | Evaluation sheet |

regulation (e.g., "I want to acquire disciplinary knowledge in English for future use") (Cronbach's α = .78, .78), EMI introjected regulation (e.g., "I would feel guilty if I did not take EMI") (Cronbach's α = .73, .73) and EMI external regulation (e.g., "I am taking EMI courses because I want to earn enough credits to graduate") (Cronbach's α = .72, .60) were applied. Integrated regulation was not included as the same reasons explained in Chapter 3 (Noels et al., 2000; Vallerand et al., 1989) Another four items were applied to measure the degree of amotivation (e.g., "I don't understand why I have to take EMI courses.") (Cronbach's α = .80, .85).

Three items each were employed to assess the degree of fulfillment of the three psychological needs which influence EMI intrinsic motivation. Items such as "Teachers in EMI courses ask for students' opinions about the content and/or procedure of the class" were used to measure the degree of fulfillment of the need for autonomy (Cronbach's α = .63, .77). Items such as "I feel a sense of accomplishment in EMI classes" were employed to assess the degree of satisfaction of the need for competence (Cronbach's α = .75, .67). Finally, items such as "I get along with my classmates in EMI courses" reflected the degree of satisfaction with the need for relatedness (Cronbach's α = .75, .74).

Regarding the variables related to motivation to learn English, motivational intensity (intended effort) to learn English was measured with four items (Cronbach's α = .68, 74) taken from Ryan (2008) and Yashima (2002) (e.g., "If English were not taught in school, I would try to go to English classes somewhere else"). Participants were required to indicate the degree to which they agreed with each statement. Four items reflected students' attitudes to learning English (Cronbach's α = .81, 86), such as "I really enjoy learning English." These were taken from Ryan (2009). The items for the ideal L2 self and ought-to L2 self of the L2 motivational self system were adapted from Ryan (2009). Four items were employed to evaluate the ideal L2 self; that is, how vividly one visualizes their future ideal self as an English speaker (Cronbach's α = .80, .90), such as "I often imagine myself as someone who is able to speak English." Three items measured the ought-to L2 self, which implies someone's beliefs of what they think they ought to become (Cronbach's α = .62, .71), such as "Hardly anyone really cares whether I learn English or not."

Motivational intensity to learn content was measured with three items (Cronbach's α = .76, .92). These items were taken from the ones that Ryan (2009) and Yashima (2002) utilized to assess intended effort to learn the content of the course. To illustrate, "English" was replaced with "this subject," as in "I often think about this subject or the content that I learned from this class."

Students reported their average percentage of understanding of the EMI lecture three times (at Times 1, 2, and 3), as well as average self-study time per week in minutes (at Times 2 and 3).

On the post-questionnaire, students were asked to evaluate the pedagogical interventions implemented in class on a 6-point Likert scale (1 = *It was not useful at all*; 6 = *It was very useful*). There were three items to assess the pedagogical interventions: conducting the feedback session in Lesson 7, assigning everyone to small groups, and providing discussion forums throughout the quarter. Students could also select "I do not know" because they may have been absent when a specific educational intervention was conducted.

At the end of the preparatory tutorial session for the final exam, each student reported what they thought of it. The same 6-point Likert scale as that used for the evaluation of the pedagogical interventions on the post-questionnaire was employed.

The data were analyzed using SPSS 23. Before examining whether the series of pedagogical interventions enhanced the students' EMI intrinsic motivation, for each variable, Kolmogorov-Smirnov tests were conducted to assess normal distribution, skewness, and kurtosis (see Tables 5.2, 5.3, 5.4, and 5.5). The results of Time 1 indicated normal distribution for EMI amotivation, EMI introjected regulation, EMI identified regulation, the need for competence, the need for relatedness, attitude to learning English, ideal L2 self, ought-to L2 self, and intended effort to learn content; on the other hand, the violation of normal distribution was indicated by EMI external regulation, EMI intrinsic motivation, the need for autonomy, and intended effort to learn English. The outcomes of Time 3 indicated normal distribution for EMI amotivation, EMI introjected regulation, EMI identified regulation, EMI intrinsic motivation, the need for autonomy, the need for relatedness, attitude to learning English, intended effort to learn English, ought-to L2 self, and intended effort to learn content. On the contrary, a violation of normal distribution was found for EMI external regulation, the need for competence, and ideal L2 self. Since some factors violated the assumption of normality, both *t*-tests and Wilcoxon rank-sum tests were carried out for RQ1, RQ2 and RQ3. The results of the paired *t*-tests will be discussed here because parametric and non-parametric tests showed the same findings.

In addition, the student evaluations of the educational interventions in the post-questionnaire were analyzed with descriptive statistics. A two-way repeated measures analysis of variance (ANOVA) was conducted to answer RQ4. As it was important to take a closer look at the data, students were divided into three groups based on their EMI intrinsic motivational trajectories (i.e., the ascent group, the descent group, and the stable group). A two-way ANOVA was then carried out to examine the statistical differences of EMI intrinsic motivation among the groups in both the pre- and post-questionnaires. The analysis confirmed that there are three types of motivational trajectories among the participants: students whose EMI intrinsic motivation scores rose (the ascent group), those whose scores fell (the descent group), and those whose scores did not change (the stable group). This process aimed to understand participants in a similar way to the cluster analyses performed in previous research on language classrooms (e.g., Hiromori, 2006; Maekawa & Yashima, 2012; Tanaka & Hiromori, 2007).

### Results

Before the research questions were answered, descriptive statistics were recorded (see Tables 5.2, 5.3, 5.4, and 5.5).

Paired $t$-tests were done to investigate the effectiveness of the pedagogical interventions. After Bonferroni correction, unfortunately, intended effort to learn content ($t$ (37) = .14, $p$ <.05, $\eta^2$ =.14) declined. No significant change was found in any other variables between Times 1 and 3. To answer RQ3 one-way ANOVA was performed. There was a significant decrease between Times 1 and 3 ($F$ [2, 64] = 4.46, $p$ < .05, $\eta^2$ = .12) in terms of self-reporting of their understanding of the lectures. There was no significant change between Times 1 and 2 or between Times 2 and 3 in participants' self-reported understanding of the lectures. Average self-study time per week dropped between Times 2 and 3 ($t$ [34] = 3.46, $p$ < .01, $\eta^2$ = .26).

Although the analyses did not indicate any positive changes on average before or after the series of pedagogical interventions, the evaluation suggested that students believed that it benefitted their learning. According to the results of the descriptive statistics, 84 percent of the participants said that belonging to a small, fixed group with international students was *somewhat useful* or *very useful* for their learning. Additionally, 67 percent of the participants saw the discussion forums in English as *useful*, and 66 percent expressed that the feedback session in Lesson 7 was *useful*. Although only 11 of the participants joined the tutorial, everyone said it was *somewhat* to *very useful* in preparing them for the final exam.

To answer RQ4, the students were divided into an ascent group ($N$ = 15), a descent group ($n$ = 14), and a stable group ($n$ = 8) based

*Table 5.2* Descriptive statistics for each factor at Time 1 (Pre-Survey)

| Variable | | Mean | SD | Sig Kolmogorov-Smirnov test | Skewness | Kurtosis |
|---|---|---|---|---|---|---|
| | Amotivation | 2.62 | 1.15 | .200 | .57 | .15 |
| | External regulation | 3.83 | 1.16 | .000 | -1.07 | 1.16 |
| Motivational regulations for EMI | Introjected regulation | 3.42 | 1.15 | .105 | -.08 | .31 |
| | Identified regulation | 4.22 | 1.03 | .200 | -.53 | .50 |
| | Intrinsic motivation | 3.70 | 1.13 | .032 | .46 | .16 |
| | Need for autonomy | 3.32 | 1.03 | .000 | .43 | .00 |
| The three psychological needs[a] | Need for competence | 3.59 | 1.09 | .200 | -.01 | -.16 |
| | Need for relatedness | 3.98 | 1.21 | .200 | -.03 | -.75 |
| | Attitude to learning English | 4.29 | 1.06 | .200 | -.46 | .83 |
| Motivational variables for learning English | Intended effort to learn English | 3.59 | .97 | .028 | .74 | 1.00 |
| | Ideal L2 self | 4.11 | 1.17 | .200 | -.15 | -.61 |
| | Ought-to L2 self | 4.46 | .94 | .178 | -.14 | -.37 |
| Motivational variable for learning content | Intended effort to learn content | 4.37 | 1.06 | .065 | -.40 | -.22 |

[a] Represents the fulfillment of the three psychological needs within SDT.

*Table 5.3* Descriptive statistics for each factor at Time 3 (Post-Survey)

| Variable | | Mean | SD | Sig Kolmogorov-Smirnov test | Skewness | Kurtosis |
|---|---|---|---|---|---|---|
| Motivational regulations for EMI | Amotivation | 2.91 | 1.10 | .086 | -.17 | -.44 |
| | External regulation | 4.02 | 1.14 | .004 | -1.03 | 1.17 |
| | Introjected regulation | 3.51 | 1.23 | .104 | -.40 | -.58 |
| | Identified regulation | 4.06 | 1.03 | .200 | -.48 | -.09 |
| | Intrinsic motivation | 3.74 | 1.01 | .200 | -.16 | 1.02 |
| The three psychological needs [a] | Need for autonomy | 3.58 | 1.14 | .200 | -.07 | -.52 |
| | Need for competence | 3.37 | .97 | .040 | .30 | .36 |
| | Need for relatedness | 4.02 | 1.11 | .071 | -.22 | -.40 |
| Motivational variables for learning English | Attitude to learning English | 4.32 | 1.09 | .200 | -.30 | -.48 |
| | Intended effort to learn English | 3.54 | 1.06 | .200 | .30 | -.25 |
| | Ideal L2 self | 4.16 | 1.30 | .049 | -.17 | -1.13 |
| | Ought-to L2 self | 3.94 | 1.17 | .200 | -.31 | -.18 |
| Motivational variable for learning content | Intended effort to learn content | 3.97 | 1.32 | .200 | -.18 | -.75 |

Note:
[a] Represents the fulfillment of the three psychological needs within SDT.

*Table 5.4* Descriptive statistics for participants' self-reported understanding of the EMI lectures

| Variable | | Mean | SD | Sig Kolmogorov-Smirnov test | Skewness | Kurtosis |
|---|---|---|---|---|---|---|
| Self-reported understanding of the lectures (%) | Time 1 | 74.19 | 14.38 | .004 | .18 | .12 |
| | Time 2 | 68.87 | 16.32 | .019 | -.17 | -.52 |
| | Time 3 | 66.13 | 13.65 | .000 | -.48 | -.56 |

*Table 5.5* Descriptive statistics for self-study time per week

| Variable | | Mean | SD | Sig Kolmogorov-Smirnov test | Skewness | Kurtosis |
|---|---|---|---|---|---|---|
| Self-study time per week (minutes) | Time 2 | 78.87 | 59.37 | .000 | 1.01 | .54 |
| | Time 3 | 55.81 | 53.54 | .001 | 1.35 | 1.55 |

*Table 5.6* Score of EMI intrinsic motivation for each group

| | Ascent group (n = 15) | | Descent group (n = 14) | | Stable group (n = 8) | | Total | |
|---|---|---|---|---|---|---|---|---|
| | Mean | SD | Mean | SD | Mean | SD | Mean | SD |
| Time 1 | 3.07 | 0.68 | 4.11 | 1.30 | 4.19 | 0.99 | 3.70 | 1.13 |
| Time 3 | 3.73 | 0.70 | 3.50 | 1.25 | 4.19 | 0.99 | 3.74 | 1.01 |

on their EMI intrinsic motivation trajectories between Times 1 and 3 (see Table 5.6 and Figure 5.1). A two-way ANOVA confirmed that a simple main effect of time was significant for both the ascent group ($F$ [1,34] = 29.07, $p$ < .001, $\eta^2$ = .50) and the descent group ($F$[1,34] = 22.50, $p$ < .001, $\eta^2$ = .79). The results also revealed a significant group difference at Time 1 ($F$[2,34] = 4.92, $p$ < .05, $\eta^2$ = .23). In addition, the interaction of group by time was statistically significant ($F$[2, 34] = 25.65, $p$ < .001, $\eta^2$ = .44). A Bonferroni multiple comparison was carried out; compared to both the descent ($p$ < .05) and the stable ($p$ < .05) groups at Time 1, the ascent group had statistically lower EMI intrinsic motivation. There was no significant difference in EMI intrinsic motivation among the groups at Time 3. This implies that students who had low EMI intrinsic motivation at the beginning demonstrated an increase and that some who were already highly motivated initially were able to sustain their EMI intrinsic motivation, while others displayed a decrease in it.

To grasp the differences among the groups of students with different motivational trajectories in other variables, a two-way repeated measures ANOVA was carried out. The findings revealed a significant difference in the descent group between Times 1 and 2 regarding participants' self-reporting of their understanding of the lectures ($F$[2, 58] = 8.61, $p$ < .01, $\eta^2$ = .13). Their mean score for self-reporting of their understanding of the EMI lectures at Time 1 was 80 percent ($SD$ = 15.49), while at Time 2, it was 68 percent ($SD$ = 22.12). This suggested that the descent group students' understanding at Time 2 was statistically lower than at Time 1. Moreover, the results revealed a significant difference for the stable group between Times 1 and 3 in self-reporting of their understanding of the lectures ($F$[2,58] = 9.76, $p$ < .01, $\eta^2$ = .14). Their mean score of the understanding of the lectures at Time 1 was 71.88 percent ($SD$ = 13.08), while at Time 3 it was 56.25 percent ($SD$ = 14.20). This implied that the stable group students' self-reported comprehension of the EMI lectures at Time 3 was significantly lower than at Time 1. In contrast, no significant difference was found for the ascent group, which underlines the importance of a sense of understanding in enhancing EMI intrinsic motivation.

## Discussion

The results show that the average scores did not change for EMI intrinsic motivation, EMI extrinsic motivation, EMI amotivation or for the three psychological needs. Although there was no statistical difference, fulfillment of the need for competence decreased slightly. Unfortunately, intended effort to learn content decreased even with carefully planned

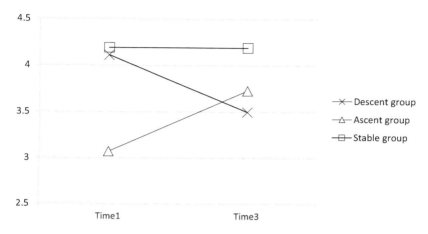

*Figure 5.1* EMI intrinsic motivation for each group at Times 1 and 3.

various pedagogical interventions. These results may seem negative; however, it is possible that students' motivation would have declined drastically without the pedagogical interventions. Prior research on English-language classrooms indicates that students lose their motivation as they continue studying English, with the initial excitement of learning diminishing over time (Johnson, 2013). In addition, there are several reasons why students might lose their motivation to learn English. Hayashi (2012) conducted retrospective interviews with Japanese university students to explore their motivational trajectory. The results reveal that students' intrinsic motivation to learn English declined when classes became too difficult. Not knowing how to study also heightened amotivation. Johnsons' qualitative study (2013) of Japanese university students, which is in line with Hayashi's study (2012) reported that one of the reasons why students' intended effort to learn English falls during university studies is a lack of self-efficacy in English ability. These findings of the previous research above (Johnson, 2013; Hayashi, 2012) expressed the importance of satisfaction of the need for competence and self-confidence in learning. As described in this book, Japanese students' self-efficacy is extremely low because of the significantly challenging nature of EMI. This leads to substandard evaluation from the EMI disciplinary instructors and international students. Thus, the results could imply that the series of pedagogical interventions at least maintained EMI intrinsic motivation and the three psychological needs (i.e., the needs for autonomy, competence, and relatedness).

Conversely, there is also room to argue that the pedagogical interventions were probably not as effective as expected. There are several possible explanations for this. First, the content of the first class (Time 1) was class orientation, such as explaining the syllabus, and did include a little content about gender studies, this made the first class a little easier for the students to follow. Naturally, though, as the course progressed, the content of the lectures became more complex, resulting in a considerable decrease in the satisfaction of students' need for competence on the post-questionnaire. Another reason why the pedagogical interventions might not be as influential as hoped was that I did not teach the course, and thus did not control lesson plans, classroom materials, or even the timings for the data collection, unlike numerous prior studies in language classrooms (Agawa & Takeuchi, 2017; Hiromori, 2006; Maekawa & Yashima, 2012; Nishida, 2013; Tanaka & Hiromori, 2007).

Although comparing the average scores of each factor between the pre- and post-surveys seems to produce negative results, exploring the trajectories of individuals shows that 40 percent of the participants increased their EMI intrinsic motivation, and 20 percent maintained high EMI intrinsic motivation. In fact, previous interventional studies in language classrooms have only succeeded in enhancing approximately 20 percent of participants' motivation. For example, in Tanaka and Hiromori's (2007) study, 26 percent of the participants increased their intrinsic motivation to learn English. In Maekawa and Yashima (2012), 22 percent of the participants increased theirs. The exception is Hiromori (2006), in which intrinsic motivation increased in 68 percent of the participants. Even in his study, students who were already intrinsically motivated maintained the same level of intrinsic motivation. In those previous studies, a group of students who dropped their motivation did not exist, therefore the average score of the participants tended to change positively, unlike this current study. Although a way to stop students from losing their EMI motivation has to be uncovered, comparing these results in English language classrooms with the current study, with 234 students in one classroom, boosting EMI intrinsic motivation in 40 percent of participants can be perceived as evidence of the pedagogical interventions' success.

Finally, the period in which the interventions and data collection were carried out was very short. Former interventional studies in language classrooms took longer to complete the intervention and data collection. For example, Yashima et al. (2018) took 15 weeks, and Hiromori (2006) took 12 weeks. Some other interventional studies even took a full academic year to complete theirs (Agawa & Takeuchi, 2017; Maekawa & Yashima, 2012). In contrast, this study only had seven weeks to complete the interventions and data collection. This time restriction made it extremely challenging to see the statistical change by which to measure the interventions' effectiveness.

## The effect of the pedagogical interventions: Dependent on motivational profiles

The quantitative study in this chapter explored the impact of the series of pedagogical interventions in Gender Studies to enhance student comprehension of the lectures and fulfill three psychological needs within SDT to boost their EMI motivation. Although the average score of EMI intrinsic motivation did not change after the series of the pedagogical interventions, it made it clear that participants who were not initially motivated demonstrated an increase in their EMI intrinsic motivation. Others with an initially high level of EMI intrinsic motivation maintained it; however, some participants experience a decline in their EMI intrinsic motivation, even with the pedagogical interventions. The results also showed that a group of the students who increased their EMI intrinsic motivation sustained their perceived understanding of the EMI lectures throughout the course, while others felt that lectures became more demanding to follow as the course progressed. It confirmed that a sense of self-efficacy is critical for students to be motivated. The overall results can be interpreted positively compared to previous interventional studies in language classrooms, but this cannot be decisively concluded due to the lack of a control group. Therefore, Study 4, a qualitative study, was conducted to compensate for the limitation.

## References

Agawa, T., & Takeuchi, O. (2017). Pedagogical intervention to enhance self-determined forms of L2 motivation: Applying self-determination theory in the Japanese university EFL context. *Language Education & Technology, 54*, 135–166.

Hayashi, H. (2012). *Doukizukeshitende miru nihonjinno eigo gakushu: Naihatsuteki gaihatsutekidoukizukewo jikuni* [English learning among Japanese students from motivational perspectives: Intrinsic and extrinsic motivation as core elements]. Kinseido.

Hiromori, T. (2006). The effects of educational intervention on L2 learners' motivational development. *JACET Bulletin, 43*, 1–14.

Johnson, M. P. (2013). A longitudinal perspective on EFL learning motivation in Japanese engineering students. In M. T. Apple, D. D. Silva, & T. Fellner (Eds.), *Language learning motivation in Japan* (pp. 189–205). Multilingual Matters. https://doi.org/10.21832/9781783090518-013

Maekawa, Y., & Yashima, T. (2012). Examining the motivational effect of presentation-based instruction on Japanese engineering students: From the viewpoints of the ideal self and self-determination theory. *Language Education & Technology*, *49*, 65–92. https://doi.org/10.24539/let.49.0_65

Malcolm, D. (2013). Motivational challenges for Gulf Arab students studying medicine in English. In E. Ushioda (Ed.), *International perspectives on motivation: Language learning and professional challenges* (pp. 98–116). Palgrave Macmillan. https://doi.org/10.1057/9781137000873_6

Nishida, R. (2013). *Empirical studies of affective variables and motivational changes among Japanese elementary school EFL learners*. Kinseido.

Noels, K. A., Pelletier, L. G., Clément, R., & Vallerand R. J. (2000). Why are you learning a second language? Motivational orientations and self-determination theory. *Language Learning*, *50*(1), 57–85. https://doi.org/10.1111/0023-8333.00111

Reeve, J. (2002). Self-determination theory applied to educational settings. In E. L. Deci & R. M. Ryan (Eds.), *Handbook of self-determination research* (pp. 183–203). Rochester, NY: University of Rochester Press.

Ryan, S. (2008). *The ideal L2 selves of Japanese learners of English* [Unpublished doctoral dissertation]. University of Nottingham. http://eprints.nottingham.ac.uk/10550/1/ryan-2008.pdf

Ryan, S. (2009). Self and identity in L2 motivation in Japan: The ideal L2 self and Japanese learners of English. In Z. Dörnyei & E. Ushioda (Eds.), *Motivation, language identity and the L2 self* (pp. 120–143). Multilingual Matters. https://doi.org/10.21832/9781847691293-007

Ryan, R. M., & Powelson, C. L. (1991). Autonomy and relatedness as fundamental to motivation and education. *Journal of Experimental Education*, *60*(1), 49–66. https://doi.org/10.1080/00220973.1991.10806579

Tanaka, H., & Hiromori, T. (2007). The effects of educational intervention that enhances intrinsic motivation of L2 students. *JALT Journal*, *29*(1), 59–80. https://doi.org/10.37546/JALTJJ29.1-3

Vallerand, R. J., Blais, M. R., Briére, N. M., & Pelletier, J. G. (1989). Construction et validation de l'Echelle de motivation en education (EME) [Construction and validation of the Motivation toward Education Scale]. *Canadian Journal of Behavioral Science / Revue canadienne des sciences du comportement*, *21*(3), 323–349. https://doi.org/10.1037/h0079855

Yashima, T. (2002). Willingness to communicate in a second language: The Japanese EFL context. *The Modern Language Journal*, *86*(1), 54–66. https://doi.org/10.1111/1540-4781.00136

Yashima, T., MacIntyre, P., & Ikeda, M. (2018). Situated willingness to communicate in an L2: Interplay of individual characteristics and context. *Language Teaching Research*, *22*(1), 115–137. https://doi.org/10.1177/1362168816657851

Yashima, T., Noels, K., Shizuka, T., Takeuchi, O., Yamane, S., & Yoshizawa, K. (2009). The interplay of classroom anxiety, intrinsic motivation, and gender in the Japanese EFL context. *Kansai University Journal of Foreign Language Education and Research*, *17*, 41–64

# 6 Importance of community in enhancing motivation

## Study 4: The effect of the pedagogical interventions: Listening to students' voices

A series of pedagogical interventions, including assigning students to groups with international students, using online discussion boards in English and in Japanese were implemented in two English-medium instruction (EMI) courses. They were aiming to enhance the students' comprehension of the lectures and the three psychological needs (i.e., the need for autonomy, competence, and relatedness) within self-determination theory (SDT) and consequently motivate students. In the quantitative study discussed in Chapter 5, the interventions appeared to have some positive impact on students' motivation, although the lack of a control group means that further investigation of the effectiveness is necessary. Thus, the qualitative study described in this chapter, Study 4, investigates how the pedagogical interventions helped to increase, decrease, or maintain students' EMI intrinsic motivation from the learners' perspective.

### *Method*

Six Japanese students, one from the Gender Studies and the others from the Cultural Studies EMI courses, who participated in Study 3 and agreed to take part in the current study, were invited for interviews (see Table 6.1).

The interviews were conducted between December 2016 and March 2017. Each interview lasted between approximately 20 and 60 minutes and was conducted in Japanese. I was able to meet Jiro, Shun, and Ikumi in person, but it was difficult to meet Kai, Sae, and Wakako because of the two-month spring break immediately after the final exam for Cultural Studies. Thus, three interviews took place via Skype during the break.

To analyze the interview data, a method of analysis based partly on Corbin and Strauss (2008) and Strauss and Corbins' (1998) grounded theory approach was employed. The procedure for data analysis was as follows: (1) I transcribed spoken data and reread the transcripts; (2) data were coded sentence by sentence or based on units of meaning to create concepts, which represent the segments. As SDT is the central framework for this research, I kept SDT in mind and used the appropriate terms where relevant. (3) Concepts with similar meanings were grouped into categories; (4) steps 2 and 3 were then repeated. To hear individual students' voices, each participant's data were not combined. In this chapter, categories will be enclosed in angle brackets, << >>, concepts in square brackets, [ ], and in vivo codes in double quotes, " ".

### Results and discussion: Individual stories during the pedagogical interventions

First, some individual information collected in the survey for Study 3, which is also essential in this study, is summarized in Table 6.1. In the following section, the overall results will be discussed followed by the discussions of four cases.

All participants except Kai scored above 500 on their TOEFL ITP, and everyone passed the course. Jiro attained the highest final grade (A+) in Cultural Studies, and Ikumi got an A in Gender Studies, although her perception of comprehension of the lectures was the lowest. Kai, Shun, and Sae got Bs, while Wakako received the lowest grade, C, among the participants. She expected her final grade to be higher than a C, so she complained about it during the interview. Kai, on the other hand, nearly achieved an A (79 percent) though his TOEFL ITP score was the lowest among the participants (TOEFL ITP 450).

The time allotted per week for self-study varied among the participants, as evident in Table 6.1. The evaluation of the series of pedagogical interventions for each pedagogical approach also varied. To illustrate, Jiro, Shun, and Wakako thought that online discussion forums in English were beneficial for self-study, but Kai considered them to be a waste of time because he could read others' comments, copy what they said, and post them as if they were his ideas. Most of the participants said they enjoyed small-group discussions with international students, except for Sae, who did not enjoy them due to not having as many opportunities for speaking English as she expected.

In the next section, I will discuss four participants—Jiro, Kai, Shun, and Sae—individually. These four participants highlight the range of

Table 6.1 Individual information from Study 3

| | Jiro | Kai | Shun | Sae | Wakako | Ikumi |
|---|---|---|---|---|---|---|
| Experience of studying abroad | None (Returnee) | None | One year | Twice, one year each time | One year | None |
| TOEFL ITP | 520 | 450 | 552 | 540 | 557 | 500 |
| Grades | 2 | 4 | 4 | 3 | 3 | 2 |
| Gender | Male | Male | Male | Female | Female | Female |
| Final grades [a] | 90 (A+) | 79 (B) | 79 (B) | 78.5 (B) | 63.5 (C) | 82 (A) |
| Self-study time per week (min) | 90 | 60→45 | 30 | 60 | 30 | 20 |
| Understanding of the lectures [b] (%) | 70→80→80 | 80→70→70 | 80→60→90 | 80→90→80 | 80→70 [c] | 50→30 [c] |
| Intended effort to learn English | 5.75→4.67 | 3.25→3.33 | 4.00→3.00 | 4.25→4.00 | 3.00→3.67 | 4.25→2.75 |
| Intended effort to learn content | 6→6 | 4.33→5.00 | 4.33→3.67 | 4→3 | 3.33→4.00 | 4.67→2.67 |
| EMI intrinsic motivation | 5.50→5.25 | 3.25→4.5 | 5.50→3.75 | 4.75→4.5 | 3.75→4.25 | 3.50→4.33 |

Notes:
[a] Refers to the final grade that the students earned in the course.
[b] Represents participants' self-perception of their understanding of the lectures.
[c] Wakako and Ikumi were absent for Lesson 1. Thus, their self-perceptions of the understanding of the lectures was only assessed for lessons 7 and 14.

reactions to the series of pedagogical interventions from extremely positive to quite critical.

***Case 1 Jiro: Very positive feedback toward the pedagogical interventions.*** Jiro was the most proactive Japanese student during the pedagogical interventions. For instance, he spent the longest time for self-study among all the participants (i.e., 90 minutes per week), and was the only Japanese student who volunteered for an optional group presentation assignment. In addition, he asked questions in person after class, as well as via e-mail. He earned an A+ as his final grade in Cultural Studies.

The following comments represent his high <<EMI intrinsic motivation>>. The following quote reports how he came to enjoy Cultural Studies as the course progressed.

*Excerpt 1*

Jiro        **To be honest, at the beginning, I felt that posting my comments
            on the discussion forums every week was tiring. However,
            I realized that participating in the discussion forums fostered
            my comprehension of the lectures and increased my motivation.
            From the second or third week of the quarter, I realized that
            I was looking forward to coming to class.**

In addition, Jiro said that compared to other EMI courses he had taken before, "I can only find better things in Cultural Studies." His overall response to the pedagogical interventions was extremely positive. First of all, fulfillment of the needs for competence and relatedness in a small group was expressed. Jiro repeatedly made positive comments about his valuable experiences working with the international students in a small group. This was observed in the concepts such as [group members were close enough to collaborate on the group presentation] and [discovered good personalities of the international students through group work], classified under the category <<fulfillment of the need for relatedness>>. Moreover, some concepts such as [a sense of accomplishment through the group presentation] and [learned a new way of doing group work through the group presentation assignment], under the category <<fulfillment of the need for competence>>, show how Jiro built confidence based on positive learning experiences, in turn satisfying the need for competence (Ryan & Deci, 2002). For instance, he described how everyone quickly grew into a close relationship in his group, so they naturally agreed to volunteer for the presentation assignment together. He also talked about his intercultural experiences through the group presentation, which show fulfillment of the need for competence. At first, he wanted to prepare for the presentation along with his group members, but they preferred working individually and being responsible for their respective parts. He was uncomfortable and worried about how this would work because he had never done a group assignment in that way. However, when the presentation turned out to be successful, he realized he had learned that there was more than one way to do group work effectively. In other words, he felt [a sense of accomplishment through group presentation]. The following statement reflects how he experienced a sense of growth.

*Excerpt 2*

Jiro **In the beginning, I thought we had different preferences for how to prepare for the presentation. Yet each of us did good work when we put everything together in the end, and the overall quality of the presentation was not bad. I have learned that group work could work this way too.**

Next, Jiro's statements reveal that online discussion forums in English helped to fulfill the need for competence. Jiro had a very positive attitude toward the online discussion forums, which promoted reviewing the lectures, as evident from his responses such as [learning was improved by reviewing the lessons] through online discussion forums, [online discussion forums in English raised awareness of the value of reviewing], and [online discussion forums in English fostered reviewing]. These fall under the categories <<fulfillment of the need for competence>> and <<positive feedback on the interventions>>. As mentioned earlier, at first he felt it was tiring to post on the online discussion forums. Nevertheless, he realized that he remembered his new knowledge from the lectures until the end of the course, leading to the fulfillment of the need for competence. Jiro believed that posting comments on the online discussion forums helped him review the content of the lectures more than for other EMI courses he had taken previously, thereby developed his comprehension of the lectures.

Furthermore, Jiro considered that online discussion forums in Japanese helped to sustain EMI motivation. Sharing his negative feelings and anxiety in the online discussion forums in Japanese made him realize that everyone struggled with understanding the lectures. He added that he could maintain his self-efficacy and motivation since he knew he was not alone, which shows the fulfillment of the need for relatedness is crucial in EMI. The online discussion board made them vulnerable, but taking that risk fosters the awareness that everyone was in the same boat. The mutual nonjudgmental attitude connects them strongly and fulfills the need for relatedness and the need for autonomy. In addition, the concepts such as [knowing that the lectures were difficult for everyone helped maintain motivation] and [a relief to know that everyone struggled with understanding the lectures] under the category, <<maintaining self-efficacy>>, reveal that the online discussion forums in Japanese actually satisfy one's need for competence as well. In other words, the discussion forums in Japanese fulfill all three psychological needs and contribute to sustaining or even enhancing EMI intrinsic motivation and EMI identified regulation. The following anecdote illustrates how online discussion forums in Japanese contributed to sustaining Jiro's self-efficacy and motivation.

*Excerpt 3*

Jiro                I sometimes felt that a lecture was very difficult. Then, I saw
                    others' posts about how much they understood the lecture, and
                    I was relieved to know that their understanding was not much
                    better.

*Excerpt 4*

Jiro                I would be disappointed if I were the only one who did not
                    understand the lecture, but if it was really difficult [for everyone],
                    I thought I should review it again. Knowing that everyone is
                    struggling with EMI helped me maintain my motivation.

Finally, the interview shows that the importance of Japanese teaching assistants (TAs). They not only encourage students to ask questions but also could serve as role models for other Japanese students. Jiro said that the TAs in EMI were usually non-Japanese, so it was challenging for him to ask questions. The Japanese TAs for Cultural Studies did in fact make asking questions much more comfortable for Jiro as seen in the following statement and concepts such as [Japanese TAs were approachable and could be asked questions], [Japanese TAs were extremely helpful in EMI], and [International TAs were not approachable and could not be asked questions].

*Excerpt 5*

Jiro                There were some Japanese TAs, even though it was an EMI, so
                    I could ask questions. I hesitated to ask questions in most EMIs
                    with only international TAs.

Jiro's stories, concepts, and categories infer that he felt safe enough to be proactive in Cultural Studies. He felt connected with the members of his small group, other Japanese students, and even with the Japanese TAs. This strong sense of belonging to multiple communities in and out of class motivated him to take on the challenge of the group presentation assignment and allowed him to enjoy the learning process (i.e., the satisfaction of the need for relatedness boosted his self-efficacy and made him try his best).

*Case 2 Kai: Positive attitude toward the pedagogical interventions.* Kai could be considered a successful case of the pedagogical interventions because despite having the lowest TOEFL ITP score (450) among the participants, he received a B as his final grade, which was the same as Shun and Sae, who had studied abroad and had much higher TOEFL ITP scores. In fact, considering that TOEFL ITP 500 is a minimum score to apply for many universities in English-speaking countries, it is easy to imagine how he would have a hard time following EMI no matter how the teacher conducted the class. As expected, during his interview, Kai shared his negative learning experiencing in an EMI course he had taken before, which is represented by categories such as <<strong sense of loneliness in EMI taken before>>. On the other hand, in Cultural Studies, the interview data show that working in a small group with international students and the online discussion forums in Japanese satisfied his need for relatedness. Another interesting point in his interview is that he expressed a <<negative attitude toward using Japanese>> in EMI, even though his English proficiency was the lowest among the participants. Although it was demanding for him to follow the lectures in English, he considered EMI as a platform for Japanese and international students to learn in the same arena. Thus, he believed that the Japanese language should not be used as a medium of instruction to teach the content. His interview and the concepts therein are discussed from the following four points.

First, Kai repeatedly mentioned a strong sense of loneliness when he began to take EMI. At the time of the interview, he was about to graduate but, even during his last semester, he occasionally felt isolated in other EMI courses. Although he had accepted feeling a strong sense of loneliness as a part of EMI, he said he cried when he felt he was the only one who did not understand the lecture. The following statement expresses the strong sense of alienation in EMI.

*Excerpt 6*

Kai        **When I first started to take EMI, I felt like I was a guest who was not welcomed in class. … It was at the end of my sophomore year that I was finally able to start taking EMI, but it was like being in someone else's house uninvited, so I tended to be passive in class.**

Concepts such as ['being' a guest in someone else's house], [crying because of strong feelings of loneliness and alienation], and [passive learning behaviors due to 'being' a guest in EMI] fall under the category of <<strong sense of loneliness in EMI taken before>>, as described above.

As we can see, a student who has already spent two years on campus in his home country found the EMI environment extremely uncomfortable and alienating, which shows students unfulfillment of the need for relatedness is critical, as reported in another qualitative study in this book discussed in Chapter 4 (Study 2). In contrast, Kai felt he could relate to other Japanese students via the online discussion forums in Japanese. He realized that the online discussion forums in Japanese in EMI courses were essential because it was a community to which he could belong. Therefore, he suggested that the online discussion forums in Japanese be applied in other EMI courses as well. The following statement reflects his positive evaluation of online discussion forums in Japanese in EMI.

*Excerpt 7*

Kai         **It was quite comfortable for me to have a Japanese discussion forum where I could reflect on my learning in EMI. [I knew I had a place to go] when I was anxious about the class. Many Japanese students seemed to share their experiences and feelings there, so I think the online discussion forum in Japanese responded well to our needs in EMI.**

The concepts related to the account above are [feeling comfortable to have a place to reflect on learning in Japanese], [feeling safe to have a place to share one's anxiety and be vulnerable in Japanese], and [discussion forums in Japanese saved me from loneliness and alienation]; they fall under the category of <<fulfillment of the needs for autonomy and relatedness>>. His interview demonstrates that the online discussion forums in Japanese created a community to which he could belong. Furthermore, he did not need to be worried about being judged, which implies that the forums fulfilled his needs for autonomy and relatedness while decreasing loneliness dramatically.

In addition to the discussion forums in Japanese, a fixed small group with the international students fulfills the need for relatedness as well as the need for competence, which are represented by the concept, [feeling comfortable in a small group]. For instance, his score at midterm was worse than he had expected, which made him realize that he had not fully understood the lectures. Hence, he started to ask the international students in his group questions to catch up. After a while, he could tell that his understanding of the course content had improved, and he eventually came to enjoy the lectures, which cultivated his positive attitude toward Cultural Studies. His small group worked as a learning community and contributed to the <<fulfillment of the need for competence>>, thereby increasing EMI intrinsic motivation. In other words, the series of pedagogical interventions safeguarded him from the intimidating learning environment, and thereby, satisfied the three psychological needs.

Finally, Kai also expressed a negative attitude toward using Japanese in EMI. In fact, communicating with the international students in his group satisfied to some degree the need for competence. Nevertheless, the category <<unfulfillment of the need for competence>>, which includes the concepts such as [taking Cultural Studies reinforced difficulties in learning in English], [challenging vocabulary], and [self-awareness of low performance when taking the midterm exam] reveal that he still struggled with understanding the EMI lectures. In addition, considering his relatively low TOEFL ITP score, the EMI classes must be hard for him to follow. Still, he felt it would be unfair to the international students if Japanese were used to teach the contents of the course in EMI. He believed that the use of Japanese should be limited to students sharing their feelings and creating a better community—much like what these pedagogical interventions tried to do. He suggested that students take EMI preparatory courses if they preferred conceptual learning in Japanese. The reason why Japanese should not be used to learn course content in EMI is mentioned below.

*Excerpt 8*

Kai          **Taking EMI means that Japanese and international students learn in the same arena, so we should be treated equally. I would not agree with giving Japanese students an advantage by using Japanese in class.**

Kai's stories in this section reveal his positive attitude toward learning English, thereby contributing to his perseverance to learn in English.

***Case 3 Shun: Positive attitude toward the pedagogical interventions, but lost EMI intrinsic motivation.*** The next case, Shun had similar positive learning experiences as Kai but experienced a loss of motivation. Like Kai, Shun also had <<harsh learning experiences in EMI taken before>> and felt a strong sense of loneliness in the EMI courses, but his small group with international students prevented him from feeling alienated in Cultural Studies. In addition, he discovered the meaning of learning in English through group discussions. However, his initial EMI intrinsic motivation shifted to EMI external regulation because he became <<too busy to focus on EMI>>.

First of all, Shun felt a strong sense of loneliness in EMI, like Kai, when he was a sophomore, and had dropped out of an EMI course because he could not withstand the strong sense of loneliness. Before studying abroad, he could not initiate a conversation in English with the international students, so he did not have anyone to talk to while others participated in a discussion in an EMI course, which is expressed in a category namely <<harsh learning experiences in EMI taken before>> from concepts such as [could not join group discussions in EMI taken before] and [dropping out of EMI due to not being able to withstand being out of the loop]. Eventually, he decided to withdraw from the course. In Cultural Studies, however, he had a small group that he could belong to and thus, he did not feel left out. The pedagogical interventions saved him from feeling alienated or rejected as he had experienced before, which means that the pedagogical interventions satisfied his need for relatedness. The following account from his interview narrates a time when he compared other EMI courses he had taken before with Cultural Studies to explain how having a small group made an EMI classroom safe enough for him to study.

*Excerpt 9*

Shun          When international students are already close to each other from
              the beginning, Japanese students fall out of the loop, and there
              is no chance for us to join a group. This is why I was relieved at
              being assigned to a group that the teachers had chosen in advance.


*Excerpt 10*

Shun          In another EMI course I attended, in a huge class, the teacher
              told us to talk with our neighbors, but I could not do that when
              I was a sophomore. I thought it was going to be overwhelming
              for me if that was how the class discussions were going to happen
              throughout the semester, so I ran away.


The following statements show that in this series of pedagogical interventions in Cultural Studies not only saved Shun from feeling lonely but also provided an international community that he could belong to, which let him see the value of EMI. Further, most of the concepts under the category <<EMI intrinsic motivation>> are related to communicating with them, such as [an increase in EMI intrinsic motivation through group discussion], [excitement through group discussions with international students], and [the excitement of gaining new perspectives through group discussions]. He said that group discussions, or even just listening to others talk in a small group, were inspiring because they always gave him new perspectives.

*Excerpt 11*

Shun    They [the Indonesian girls in his group] analyzed texts from very different perspectives than mine, and it was always very eye opening and interesting.

Another statement shows the strong positive impact communicating with the international students had on him. It embodies how the experience of international contacts changed his view of EMI courses in general, based on the concepts [learning in EMI is valuable when there are interactions with international students] and [recognizing the value of learning in English through group work]. Conversely, Shun did [not see the value of EMI without interacting with international students], which falls under the category <<EMI as a place to communicate with the international students>>. Before taking Cultural Studies, Shun had thought that using Japanese as a medium of instruction would be better, since it was faster to learn. In most EMI courses he had taken at University A before, there were no group discussions or group activities with international students, so he did not see the value of pushing himself to learn in EMI. However, in Cultural Studies, he felt that communicating with the international students in his group broadened his mind, and he wanted to recommend that everyone take Cultural Studies in English, rather than in Japanese. The following statements show that his three psychological needs of SDT were satisfied in group discussions and that he felt enjoyment and saw the value of EMI.

*Excerpt 12*

Shun    Cultural Studies was good. I would recommend to others that they take the course in English, not Japanese.

*Excerpt 13*

Shun    They [the Indonesian girls in his group] listened to my opinions very carefully. They were also honest in telling me when they did not understand my opinions. Everyone was close in my group, and it was fun.

The accounts in this category show that giving opportunities to experience realistic international contact could help to image one's ideal L2 self clearly and internalize the meaning of the study, and thereby achieve higher English proficiency. Shun became eager to exchange his opinions with the international students the same way he did with Japanese students, which was his ideal L2 self. That is why he was frustrated whenever he felt he was not yet the English speaker he wants to become. The following paragraph will elaborate how he experienced a discrepancy between his present L2 self and ideal L2 self.

Shun felt frustrated that he could not show his true abilities, such as being able to contribute to discussions actively when the medium of instruction was English. He said that he could have expressed his ideas in a class discussion and taken on the challenge of presenting at the group presentation if the medium of instruction was Japanese. It shows that participating actively in EMI is demanding even for a student like him who has studied abroad and was adequately proficient in English. The following statement illustrates how his expectations about his performance in EMI were as high as for courses conducted in Japanese.

*Excerpt 14*

Shun        **When I think about myself taking classes in Japanese, I would not be that quiet. … I feel my ability [to discuss] in English is 60 or 70 percent of its equivalent in Japanese. That is why I feel irritated with myself in EMI because I know I can do more.**

*Excerpt 15*

Shun        **To be honest, I am angry at myself that my performance is worse in EMI than in courses conducted in Japanese.**

Such a struggle could also be observed in the category <<discrepancy between ideal L2 self and present L2 self>>, which includes concepts such as [frustration at being unable to show one's real abilities in discussions in EMI], [frustration due to not being able to voice one's mind unlike in Japanese], and [wanted to lead group discussions like in discussions in Japanese]. It could explain one of the reasons why EMI intrinsic motivation did not statistically increase in the quantitative study to examine the effectiveness of the pedagogical interventions discussed in Chapter 5 (Study 3), as the ideal L2 self is an influential factor in EMI intrinsic motivation, based on the larger scale quantitative study before the pedagogical interventions reported in Chapter 3 (Study 1).

Finally, it should be mentioned that Shun experienced a decline in his EMI intrinsic motivation and was aware of his increased external regulation during the course. Shun took Cultural Studies because he was interested in the course content. However, his initial EMI intrinsic motivation gradually became extrinsic as the semester progressed because he became <<too busy to focus on EMI>>. For example, he was busy with his graduation thesis, and the company he was going to work for gave him a lot of assignments, even though he was still a student and not working there yet. He was supposed to pass the second level qualification test for bookkeeping and get a TOEIC score of 900 before starting to work for the company in April 2017 (Cultural Studies was offered from November 2016 to February 2017). Furthermore, he was already missing his university life, and therefore, his time for other things on campus and studying for the exams that he had to take (i.e., bookkeeping and TOEIC) took priority over Cultural Studies. Consequently, his focus shifted from the course, and he stopped putting effort into it. The following excerpt explains his motivational shift from intrinsic motivation to external regulation as the course continued.

*Excerpt 16*

Shun    To be honest, at first, I took Cultural Studies to gain new knowledge and a new learning experience. [Nevertheless], my goal for this course shifted to getting credits very quickly. … I spent my time and put my effort into other things for my growth and learning instead. … This was not only because of writing a graduation thesis, but also a part-time job and assignments from the company I was going to work for.

Based on the statement above, various factors outside the classroom, such as getting a job offer and working on a graduation thesis, impact EMI motivation and change learning behaviors.

*Case 4 Sae: Negative attitude toward the pedagogical interventions.* Sae blamed the pedagogical practices applied in the course for her not enjoying EMI, so she had a critical view of the series of pedagogical interventions compared to the other interviewees. She complained about the pedagogical interventions, mainly regarding the members of the small group and the use of language by the EMI disciplinary instructor. It was because she considered <<EMI as a place to practice speaking English>>, but did not have as many opportunities as she wanted in Cultural Studies. Further, understanding the course content was more challenging than she expected, which increased her frustration. Because she was confident with her English to some degree, she attributed her not being able to comprehend the content to the teachers not using Japanese.

First, Sae expressed that she was taking many EMI courses to improve her English proficiency, which is in line with some previous studies in Japan that found that language learning is a main motivation for many EMI students (Chapple, 2015; Shimauchi, 2018). She had studied abroad twice; hence, she was confident in her English proficiency to some degree but felt that she had to improve more to work internationally. This is explicit from the concepts such as [level of English proficiency not high enough to be a competitive advantage] and [level of English proficiency not high enough to be proud of]. These concepts come under the category <<discrepancy between the ideal L2 self and present L2 self>>. She was <<taking many EMI courses>> believing this would help her get closer to her ideal L2 self, which is evident from the category about <<EMI as a place to practice speaking English>>. This category includes concepts such as [taking EMI courses to have sufficient English proficiency for business], [taking many EMI courses to maintain English proficiency after studying abroad], and [taking many EMI courses for opportunities to listen to English]. That is why she was eager to use English in Cultural Studies.

However, students in her group were not willing to speak English, so Sae was very disappointed that she did not have as many chances to speak English as she expected in small group discussions. That is why she insisted that the EMI disciplinary teacher change the group. From her perspective, she could not become closer to her ideal L2 self during the term because the other members of the group did not give her opportunities to practice speaking in English. The category such as <<negative attitude toward the group>> were repeatedly mentioned, which includes the concepts [wanting instructors to change the group] and [wanting to switch her group due to it having too many Japanese speakers].

Contrary to her desire to use English in group discussions, Sae suggested that Japanese be used as the medium of instruction in EMI for conceptual learning. Like most other participants, she also faced difficulties in learning in English, based on the concepts such as [reading in English was challenging], [gaining new knowledge in English was challenging], and [did not understand the course content enough to participate in the class actively]. These ideas are classified under the category <<unfulfillment of the need for competence>>. The following statement reflects her unfulfillment of the need for competence, which made her passive in class.

*Excerpt 17*

Sae         **I did not voice my opinions freely in front of everyone or volunteer to take up the group presentation assignment because I was not confident about my understanding of the lectures.**

Interestingly, unlike Kai, Sae felt that Japanese should be used more actively to help students understand course content, although she considered EMI as a place to improve her English. This was due to feeling that it was impossible to learn in English any longer. The following statement illustrates her frustration at Japanese not being used at all in EMI.

*Excerpt 18*

Sae         **The teacher trying to explain the same thing in English a few times does not help me understand it. I will not understand it anyway. ... I wanted her to explain it in Japanese, at least once.**

Sae's desire to use Japanese in EMI is observed in the category << request for more active use of Japanese in EMI>>, which includes a wide range of concepts on the use of Japanese in EMI, such as [requesting a summary of the main points of lectures in Japanese], [requesting an explanation in Japanese and increasing the speed of the course], and [Japanese translation helps with memorizing English vocabulary].

Her opinions are almost self-contradictory, but her blaming something external and uncontrollable whenever she was not satisfied in class is consistent (e.g., reading assignment being too difficult, the other members of the group not being willing to speak in English, EMI disciplinary instructor, TAs, and my not using Japanese to help). Meanwhile, the time she dedicated for the course was only one hour per week, which was not that long. As Weiner (1992, 2010) described regarding attribution theory, individuals' interpretations of events and experiences in the past determine their future behaviors. In language learning, for example, when students consider a failure to be due to their lack of aptitude or intelligence, they tend to not continue to study, since the reasons they fail are stable and uncontrollable. Sae attributed her failure to external uncontrollable and stable factors at least during the term (i.e., EMI disciplinary instructor not using Japanese, other group members not speaking English or the reading materials being too demanding), which meant the voice in her head demotivated her. As she felt that there was nothing she could do to boost her comprehension of the lectures, or increase the opportunities to communicate with the other members of the group in English, she did not feel a sense of achievement (unfulfillment of the need for competence), of belonging (unfulfillment of the need for relatedness), or of being heard (unfulfillment of the need for autonomy).

## Three effective pedagogical approaches based on students' voices

The series of pedagogical interventions—assigning students in a small group, using online discussion forums and providing glossaries to help students follow the EMI courses—fulfill the three psychological needs, thereby enhancing student motivation. The qualitative study discussed in this chapter examines the effectiveness of the interventions, and its results reveal that the following three pedagogical approaches are especially beneficial to helping foster the participants' need for relatedness, autonomy, and competence. It also demonstrate that the need for autonomy and relatedness are fulfilled to a certain extent, while fulfillment of the need for competence is rather limited.

First, assigning Japanese students to a small group with international students is quite effective because it enhances their needs for autonomy, competence, and relatedness. To be specific, most of the participants (except Sae) felt a sense of belonging and of not being judged, so when they did not follow the lectures they could ask questions, which boosted their comprehension of the lectures. This suggests that they felt their existence was acknowledged in the community and supported by other members there. Next, the online discussion forums in Japanese enhanced their needs for relatedness and autonomy. Like Jiro and Kai, the students' motivation and self-efficacy were undermined when they assumed that everyone else understood the lectures but them. The online discussion forums in Japanese revealed that most of the Japanese students were struggling with the lectures. Sharing the anxiety and negative emotions with others gave them a place to belong to and a chance to be their true self. Finally, the online discussion forums in English fulfill the need for competence. Jiro, Shun, and Wakako mentioned that this increased their self-study time. They also read others' posts, which advanced their comprehension of the lectures. However, <<unfulfillment of the need for competence>> was mentioned by most of the participants, but not Jiro. This shows how challenging it is for Japanese students to understand lectures entirely in English. Further, Shun expressed that in EMI, the students suffer from a <<discrepancy between present L2 self and ideal L2 self>>. He was frustrated that using English was inhibiting his "true" critical thinking and discussion abilities. He believed he could have performed better if his English competence had been higher.

## References

Chapple, J. (2015). Teaching in English is not necessarily the teaching of English. *International Education Studies, 8*(3), 1–13. https://doi.org/10.5539/ies.v8n3p1.

Ryan, R. M., & Deci, E. L. (2002). An overview of self-determination theory: An organismic-dialectical perspective. In E. L. Deci & R. M. Ryan (Eds.), *Handbook of self-determination research* (pp. 3–33). University of Rochester Press.

Shimauchi, S. (2018). Gender in English-medium instruction programs: Differences in international awareness? In A. Bradford & H. Brown (Eds.), *English-medium instruction in Japanese higher education: Policy, challenges and outcomes* (pp. 180–94). Multilingual Matters. https://doi.org/10.21832/9781783098958-014

Weiner, B. (1992). *Human motivation: Metaphors, theory and research.* Sage.

Weiner, B. (2010). The development of an attribution-based theory motivation: A history of ideas. *Educational Psychologist, 45*(1), 28–36. https://doi.org/10.1080/00461520903433596

Yashima, T. (2009). International posture and the ideal L2 self in the Japanese EFL context. In Z. Dörnyei & E. Ushioda (Eds.), *Motivation, language identity and the L2 self* (pp. 144–163). Multilingual Matters. https://doi.org/10.21832/9781847691293-008

Yashima, T., & Arano, K. (2015). Understanding EFL learners' motivational dynamics: A three-level model from a dynamic systems and sociocultural perspective. In Z. Dörnyei, P. MacIntyre, & A. Henry (Eds.), *Motivational dynamics in language learning* (pp. 285–314). Multilingual Matters. https://doi.org/10.21832/9781783092574-020

# 7 Conclusion

## Future directions for pedagogy of EMI

The series of empirical studies discussed in this book was conducted with a twofold aim in mind: (1) To understand the current situation and challenges that English-medium instruction (EMI) is facing from the perspectives of Japanese students' motivation; and (2) to design and implement a series of pedagogical interventions and examine their effectiveness as possible solutions to the problems explored in the first half of this book using self-determination theory (SDT) as the framework.

### What did the studies find out?

Japanese students take EMI because they want to improve their English proficiency while gaining academic knowledge. In reality, however, students only understand about half of a lecture, which means that they constantly feel incompetent. Additionally, they feel that they are ignored and alienated in an EMI community, and thereby EMI becomes an obligation and a burden for Japanese students. A series of pedagogical interventions was carried out to transform EMI into a safe learning community, one in which Japanese students could grow.

As a result of implementing the pedagogical interventions, 40 percent of the participants who had a stable understanding of the lectures increased their EMI motivation during the pedagogical interventions. Among the several pedagogical interventions, assigning students to small groups with international students and using online discussion forums in Japanese and in English were found to be especially effective. Assigning Japanese students to small groups with international students gives them a place to belong, to ask questions when having a hard time following the class, and to be heard. Also, online discussion forums in Japanese become a community where they can share their negative emotions. Finally, discussion forums in English foster their self-study at home. However, the results of the quantitative and qualitative studies to investigate the effects of the pedagogical interventions (Study 3 and 4) also made it clear that some students still struggle with following the class and feel frustrated with the discrepancy between their ideal L2 self and their current L2 self.

## Pedagogical implications: What can teachers and universities do?

Taking the results and analyses of the studies in this book into consideration, I suggest one pedagogical implication for English language classrooms and six pedagogical implications for EMI courses.

### *Pedagogical implications for English-language classrooms at universities*

This research elucidates that, for Japanese students, EMI is demanding and requires perseverance, even in cases with well-planned pedagogical interventions. This implies that EMI requires at least high academic English proficiency (Malcolm, 2013; O'Dowd, 2018). Therefore, English classrooms must contribute toward improving students' academic English proficiency—that is, reading, listening, writing, and speaking—to enable them to follow EMI lectures. Among these skills, focusing on teaching productive skills may help improve their self-confidence and make EMI classes enjoyable. Since students who learn through EMI have harder time to effectively explain their conceptual knowledge than do students who learn in their first language (L1), even when students in EMI feel they have effectively learned. In addition, there are fewer interactions in EMI classrooms than in classrooms conducted in students' L1 (Airey, 2011; O'Dowd, 2018). Also, students want writing instruction, as mentioned in the qualitative study before the pedagogical interventions discussed in Chapter 4 (Study 2), and they also struggle with expressing their ideas during discussions, as is elaborated in the qualitative study to examine the effectiveness of the pedagogical interventions reported in Chapter 6 (Study 4). Thus, while any academic English language course may prove beneficial, tackling academic writing and speaking could help students to have more successful experiences in EMI.

### *Pedagogical implications for EMI classrooms*

First, to create a cooperative learning environment and enhance students' motivation, it is beneficial to put students in a small group (Dörnyei, 2001). The results of the studies in this book also expressed that assigning students to small groups with international students served to satisfy the students' three psychological needs (i.e., the needs for autonomy, competence, and relatedness), allowing them to be more proactive and responsible for their learning. In addition, interactions with international students, who are usually more fluent and competent in English than Japanese students, helps them visualize their ideal L2 selves more vividly, contributing to their determination (Dörnyei, 2009). Thus, creating small, fixed groups in EMI classrooms can increase language learners' excitement for learning in English and help them internalize the value of learning in EMI.

Second, utilizing online discussion forums in Japanese can build a community for Japanese students to engage with EMI courses. The data in the qualitative study to examine the impact of the series of pedagogical interventions described in Chapter 6 (Study 4) demonstrated that online discussion forums in Japanese offer a place where students can experience a sense of security and attachment by sharing their anxiety and resentment. This satisfies their need for relatedness (Ryan & Deci, 2017). Moreover, these forums become a place to interact with the EMI disciplinary teacher, teaching assistants (TAs) and the researcher/English teacher assuring the students that their opinions are heard—this satisfies their need for autonomy (Reeve, 2002). In fact, as many EMI courses are taught in a one-way lecture style, they usually do not offer opportunities to connect with others. Consequently, Japanese students assume that they are the only ones who do not understand the EMI lectures, which destroys their self-efficacy. However, the studies in this book revealed that the online discussion forums in Japanese help Japanese students recognize that others, too, are struggling with following the lectures. Thus, they attribute their difficulties in understanding the lectures to the level of the lectures, not to their level of English. This awareness helps them maintain their self-efficacy and determination (i.e., fulfillment of the need for competence).

In addition to the online discussion forums in Japanese, the last qualitative study discussed in Chapter 6 (Study 4) revealed that asking a comprehension check question each week on the online discussion forum in English increases the Japanese students' self-study time, thereby fostering their understanding of the EMI lectures (i.e., fulfillment of the need for competence). Students cultivate their comprehension of the course content by not only answering questions but also by reading other students' posts. This implies that using online discussion forums in English creates more opportunities for students to enhance their comprehension. Those three pedagogical approaches imply that giving students opportunities to communicate with each other is critical to cultivating their learning (Malcolm, 2013).

Furthermore, language instruction should be provided in EMI classrooms. The overall results of the studies in this book demonstrate the importance of attitude to learning English and ideal L2 selves in the Japanese EMI classrooms. This is in line with the previous research conducted in English-language classrooms in Japan (Ryan, 2009). In other words, as Macaro (2018) proposed, EMI falls on the English-language learning continuum. In addition, language learners who participated in Malcolm's (2013) study conducted in the Arab Gulf region insisted that a teachers' role is not limited to delivering subject-specific lectures, but extends to responding to students' problems and needs. As students want to improve their English proficiency by taking EMI (Chapple, 2015; Shimauchi, 2018), providing second-language instruction is critical for EMI to be motivating and enhance students' academic performance, even though language teaching (learning) is in theory not an objective of EMI courses. This can be achieved by providing terminological glossaries, since even students with high English proficiency struggle with terminology (Malcolm, 2013). Also, it could be done by giving students constructive feedback. In other words, EMI pedagogy should, to some degree, adopt a CLIL approach to make EMI courses more fruitful.

Besides the change in pedagogical practices, reducing EMI class size is also critical to increasing interactions and enhancing academic performance. Özerk (2001) conducted a quantitative study in bilingual schools in Oslo to examine the differences between smaller and larger classes. He reported that a smaller class size enables students to interact with their instructor—by asking questions and receiving feedback—helping them achieve high academic performance. This is also mentioned in the qualitative study exploring Japanese students' feelings before the pedagogical interventions discussed in Chapter 4 (Study 2). Here, a large class size functioned as a barrier for Japanese students voicing their opinions. In other words, a smaller class size is crucial to fulfilling the needs for competence and relatedness. Therefore, EMI classrooms should be the same size as language courses, or at least smaller than fifty students.

Finally, TAs are essential for simultaneously sustaining language learners' intellectual curiosity about English and course contents (Malcolm, 2013). Malcolm (2013), also suggested in a study conducted in an EMI program in the Arab Gulf region, that fluent speakers in both L1 and English can support the language learners. In Study 4, a qualitative study to investigate the influence of the pedagogical interventions, a participant expressed that Japanese TAs were more approachable compared to international ones, so they intentionally chose to ask Japanese TAs questions when they needed help. This means that Japanese TAs contributed to the fulfillment of the need for competence. Thus, although few Japanese universities have TAs in EMI courses, their presence will make EMI less demanding for not only the students, but also for the EMI disciplinary instructors.

## Final thoughts: A burden or a way to communicate with the world?

While conducting the studies in this book, I constantly questioned why EMI should be implemented in Japanese universities since students were dropping out of the course. This implies a loss in their motivation to learn both English and course content. In addition, Japanese students were not able follow the lectures and were hidden in the shadows of international students, who had a much richer educational background (Malcolm, 2013). In fact, EMI disciplinary instructors often blamed Japanese students' low English proficiency and passive learning attitude for this situation (Hernandez-Nanclares & Jimenez-Munoz, 2017; Macaro et al., 2019). Shockingly, some of them even said in front of the students that many of them were going to fail. However, the instructors were not even aware that their own attitude and behavior actually demotivated students (Cots, 2013; Malcolm, 2013; O'Dowd, 2018). Given their discouraging attitude and criticism toward Japanese students, EMI disciplinary instructors cannot expect Japanese students to be determined, especially when the students are aware that their teachers underestimate their intelligence, learning ability, and potential.

In fact, some EMI disciplinary instructors with a limited understanding of teaching still believe that disseminating information automatically implies *teaching* and that it then depends on the students whether they sink or swim (Malcolm, 2013). This book has attempted to suggest that EMI requires more student-centered approaches as well as a structured scaffolding to cultivate students' motivation and learning (Cots, 2013). As Ryan and Deci (2000) put it, people have "inherent growth tendencies" (p. 65), but their ability depends on the social environment. Further research must be conducted to formulate ways to teach EMI courses more effectively, helping language learners to read more materials from different perspectives, interact with students from different backgrounds, and develop their academic interests. However, when EMI can provide such authentic international experiences to learners, they can broaden their minds and become competitive in today's globalized world. Thus, I would be thrilled if this book could contribute to making that happen.

## References

Airey, J. (2011). The relationship between teaching and student learning in Swedish university physics. In B. Prisler, I. Klitgard, & A.H. Fabricius (Eds.), *Language and learning in the international university* (pp.3–19). Multilingual Matters.

Chapple, J. (2015). Teaching in English is not necessarily the teaching of English. *International Education Studies, 8*(3), 1–13. https://doi.org/10.5539/ies.v8n3p1

Cots, J. M. (2013). Introducing English-medium instruction at the university of Lleida, Spain: Intervention, beliefs and practices. In A. Doiz, D. Lasagabaster, & J. M. Sierra (Eds.), *English-medium instruction at universities* (pp. 28–44). Multilingual Matters.

Dörnyei, Z. (2001). *Motivational strategies in the language classroom*. Cambridge University Press.

Dörnyei, Z. (2009). The L2 motivational self system. In Z. Dörnyei & E. Ushioda (Eds.), *Motivation, language identity and the L2 self* (pp. 9–42). Multilingual Matters. https://doi.org/10.21832/9781847691293-003

Hernandez- Nanclares, N., & Jimenez-Munoz, A. (2017). English as a medium of instruction: evidence for language and content targets in bilingual education in economics. *International Journal of Bilingual Education and Bilingualism, 20*(7), 883–896. https://doi.org/10.1080/13670050.2015.1125847

Macaro, D., Jimenez-Munoz, A., & Lasagabaster, D. (2019). The importance of certification of English Medium Instruction teachers in higher education in Spain. *Porta Linguarum, 32*, 103–118.

Macaro, E. (2018). *English medium instruction*. Oxford University Press.

Malcolm, D. (2013) Motivational challenges for Gulf Arab students studying medicine in English. In E. Ushioda (Ed.), *International perspectives on motivation: Language learning and professional challenges.* (pp. 98–116). Palgrave Macmillan.

O'Dowd, R. (2018). The training and accreditation of teachers for English medium instruction: An overview of practice in European universities. *International Journal of Bilingual Education and Bilingualism, 21*(5), 553–563. https://doi.org/10.1080/13670050.2018.1491945

Özerk, K. (2001). Teacher-student verbal interaction and questioning, class size and bilingual students' academic performance. *Scandinavian Journal of Educational Research*, 45(4), 353–367.

Reeve, J. (2002). Self-determination theory applied to educational settings. In E. L. Deci & R. M. Ryan (Eds.), *Handbook of self-determination research* (pp. 183–203). University of Rochester Press.

Ryan, R. M., & Deci, E. L. (2000). Self-determination theory and the facilitation of intrinsic motivation, social development, and well-being. *American*

*Psychologist*,    *55*(1),    68–78.    https://doi.org/10.1037/0003-066x.55.1.68. https://doi.org/10.1057/9781137000873_6

Ryan, R. M., & Deci, E. L. (2017). *Self-determination theory: Basic psychological needs in motivation, development, and wellness.* Guilford Press.

Ryan, S. (2009). Self and identity in L2 motivation in Japan: The ideal L2 self and Japanese learners of English. In Z. Dörnyei & E. Ushioda (Eds.), *Motivation, language identity and the L2 self* (pp. 120–143). Multilingual Matters. https://doi.org/10.21832/9781847691293-007

Shimauchi, S. (2018). Gender in English-medium instruction programs: Differences in international awareness? In A. Bradford & H. Brown (Eds.), *English-medium instruction in Japanese higher education: Policy, challenges and outcomes* (pp. 180–194). Multilingual Matters. https://doi.org/10.21832/9781783098958-014

# Index

*Note*: Page numbers in *italics* indicate figures and in **bold** indicate tables on the corresponding pages.

Amotivation 21, **21**, 31–33, **34**, **37**, **41**, 56, 77, 80–81, **83**–**84**, 86–87
autonomy-supportive teaching approaches in EMI **55**, 65

Cenoz, J. 5
Chapple, J. 16, 45
communication with international students 67–68, 112–113
community in student motivation: listening to students' voices 91–106, **93**; negative attitude toward the pedagogical interventions 103–105; positive attitude with lost intrinsic motivation 99–103; positive attitude toward pedagogical interventions 97–99; very positive feedback toward pedagogical interventions 94–97
content and language integrated learning (CLIL) 2–4, 11
content-based instruction (CBI) 4–6
Corbin, J. 52, 92
crossroad model 15
Csikszentmihalyi, M. 1

Deci, E. L. 19–21, **21**, 36, 46, 52
Dejima model 15
Dörnyei, Z. 16, 19, 22–23

English: as barrier to belonging **52**, 55–56; as barrier to learning 50–54, **51**

English-medium instruction (EMI) 3; aims of the book and data collection procedure on 6–7; as a burden **55**, 63, 112–113; compared to CBI/CLIL 3–4; contextual background on 7–9; defining 3–4; extrinsic motivation in 19–21, **21**; gap between expectations and reality of classrooms for 23–24; harsh environment of 52–66, **53**–**55**; heavy workload in **55**, 63–64; importance of autonomy-supportive teaching approaches in **53**, 63; interactive 64–65; lack of interactions in **54**, 64; motivation in (*see* motivation in EMI); pedagogical implications for 109–112; as prerequisite to graduate 8–9
external regulation 21, **21**, 32–33, **34**, **37**, 81, **83**–**84**, 100, 103
extrinsic motivation, 19–21, **21**

Gao, X. 13
global citizen model 15
*global jinzai* 23
glossaries for reading 68–69

Hayashi, H. 87
heavy workload in EMI **55**, 63–64
Hiromori, T. 21, 31, 46, 78, 88

ideal L2 self 19, 22–24, 32, 33, **34–35**, 36–39, **37–38**, *40*, **41**, 44, 46, 77, 80–81, **83–84**, 102, 104, 109
identified regulation 21, **21**, 30, 32, **37**, 78, 80, **83–84**
integrated regulation 21, **21**, 32, **37**, 80
interactive EMI 68
intrinsic motivation in **37**, 77–78, 81–82
introjected regulation 21, **21**, 32, 80–81, **83–84**

Japanese students: designing pedagogical interventions for 66–69; desire to access PowerPoint slides for self-study 68; desire to ask questions in Japanese 69; desire to communicate with international students 67; desire for interactive EMI 68; desire to obtain glossaries for reading 68–69; desire to receive academic writing instruction 67–68; listening to voices of 91–106, **93**; necessity of pedagogical interventions for 69–70; need for autonomy, competence, and relatedness in 50–66
Japanese universities, perceptions of and motivations for EMI in 14–16
Joe, Y. 14
Johnson, M. P. 87

L2 motivational self system 19, 22–23
large class size as barrier to learning **55**, 65–66
Lee, H. K. 14

Macaro, D. 44, 111
Maekawa, Y. 22, 88
Malcolm, D. 111
Markus, H. 22
motivation in EMI: in case of University A 18–19; changing orientations with pedagogical interventions 76–88, **79**, **83–84**, *87*; community in (*see* community in student motivation); defining 16–17; gap between expectations

and reality of EMI classrooms 23–24; L2 motivational self system 19, 22–23; need for autonomy, competence, and relatedness in 50–66; overseas perceptions of 13–14; perceptions of in Japanese universities 14–16; positive attitude toward pedagogical inteventions, but lost 99–103; quantitative study to uncover 30–47; research in second language acquisition (SLA) 17; self-determination theory (SDI) 17, 19–21, **21**; significance of, and need for competence and relatedness in 47

need for autonomy 19–20; competence, and relatedness **55**, 64; EMI as a burden **55**, 64; English as barrier to belonging **53–54**, 58; English as barrier to learning 56–57, **53**; heavy workload in EMI courses **55**, 63–64; importance of autonomy-supportive teaching approaches in EMI **55**, 65; lack of self-efficacy **54**, 57; large class size as barrier to learning **55**, 65–66; method in 50–52, **51**; need for autonomy unfulfilled **54**, 61–63; need for relatedness unfulfilled **54**, 59–61; results and discussion of 52–66, **53–55**; unfulfilled **54–55**, 61–63
need for competence 20, 46–47; pedagogical interventions and need for 74–76
need for relatedness 20, 46–47; pedagogical interventions 76; unfulfilled **54–55**, 59–61
Noels, K. A. 31, 78
Nurius, P. 22

organismic integration theory (OIT) 21
ought-to L2 self 19, 22–24, 32–36, **34–34**, 77, **83–84**
Özerk, K. 111

pedagogical interventions 72–73; based on students' voices

106–107; changing motivational orientations with 76–88, **79**, **83–84**, *86*; designed based on comments from Japanese students 66–69; implications of 109–111; listening to students' voices 91–106, **93**; motivational profiles and effect of 88–89; necessity of 69–70; negative attitude toward 103–106; from perspective of SDT 73–76; positive attitude toward 97–99; lost EMI intrinsic motivation with 99–103; very positive feedback toward 94–97
PowerPoint slides 68

quantitative study of EMI motivation: discussion of 42–44, *43*; method in 30–33; results of 33–44, **34–35**, **37–39**, *40*, **41**, *42–43*, **44**
question asking in Japanese 69–70

Ryan, R. M. 19–21, **21**, 31, 32, 33, 36, 46, 52, 80

second language acquisition (SLA) 17
self-determination theory (SDT) 17, 19–22, **21**, 30, 72; changing motivational orientations with pedagogical interventions 76–89, **79**, **83–85**, *87*; listening to students' voices 91–106, **93**; pedagogical interventions from perspective of 73–76; *see also* quantitative study of EMI motivation
self-efficacy, lack of **54**, 57–59
Shimauchi, S. 15–16, 45
Strauss, A. 52, 92
Sylvén, L. K. 5

Tanaka, H. 22, 31, 46, 88
Thompson, A. S. 5
TOEFL ITP (Test of English as a Foreign Language) 8, 14, 18, 19, 31, 33, **34**, 36, 44, **51**, 57, 78, 92, **93**, 97, 99

Ushioda, E. 16

Yashima, T. 22, 31, 32, 33, 78, 80, 88